T0328603

# Cambridge Elements

### Elements in the Renaissance
edited by
John Henderson
*Birkbeck, University of London, and Wolfson College, University of Cambridge*
Jonathan K. Nelson
*Syracuse University Florence, and Kennedy School, Harvard University*

# MEASURING
# IN THE RENAISSANCE

## *An Introduction*

Emanuele Lugli
*Stanford University*

## CAMBRIDGE
UNIVERSITY PRESS

Shaftesbury Road, Cambridge CB2 8EA, United Kingdom

One Liberty Plaza, 20th Floor, New York, NY 10006, USA

477 Williamstown Road, Port Melbourne, VIC 3207, Australia

314–321, 3rd Floor, Plot 3, Splendor Forum, Jasola District Centre, New Delhi – 110025, India

103 Penang Road, #05–06/07, Visioncrest Commercial, Singapore 238467

Cambridge University Press is part of Cambridge University Press & Assessment, a department of the University of Cambridge.

We share the University's mission to contribute to society through the pursuit of education, learning and research at the highest international levels of excellence.

www.cambridge.org
Information on this title: www.cambridge.org/9781009073974

DOI: 10.1017/9781009072830

First published 2023

A catalogue record for this publication is available from the British Library.

ISBN 978-1-009-07397-4 Paperback
ISSN 2631-9101 (online)
ISSN 2631-9098 (print)

# Measuring in the Renaissance
# An Introduction

Elements in the Renaissance

DOI: 10.1017/9781009072830
First published online: June 2023

Emanuele Lugli
*Stanford University*
**Author for correspondence:** Emanuele Lugli, elugli@stanford.edu

**Abstract:** During the Renaissance, measuring played a critical role in shaping trade, material production, warfare, legal studies, and even our understanding of the heavens and hell. This Element delves into the applications of measuring, with a particular emphasis on the Italian states, and traces its wide-ranging cultural effects. The homogenization of measurements was endorsed as a means to achieve political unity. The careful retrieval of ancient standards instilled a sense of connection and ownership toward the past. Surveying was fundamental in the process of establishing colonies. This Element not only examines the perceived advantages of measuring, but it also highlights the overlooked distorting aspect of this activity. Measuring was not just a neutral quantification process but also a creative one. By suppressing or emphasizing information about the material world, measuring influenced people's perceptions and shaped their ideas about what was possible and what could be accomplished.

**Keywords:** Renaissance Italy, history of measuring, Renaissance art history, early modern history, Renaissance art

ISBNs: 9781009073974 (PB), 9781009072830 (OC)
ISSNs: 2631-9101 (online), 2631-9098 (print)

# Contents

# 1 Warnings

## 1.1 Under the Loggia

It is market day, and you have been tasked to buy grains. As usual, you and the seller meet under the loggia, where a measurer stands next to a *staio*, a bucket-like standard for dry goods. If you were in late sixteenth-century Norcia, the officer would pour the cereals into the cylinders carved in stone adjacent to the Church of San Benedetto (Figure 1), three of which survived the 2016 earthquake as well as the catastrophes of the previous 400 years (Patrizi-Forti 1869: 514). You are in fifteenth-century Florence, however, and the measurer uses a metal *staio*, which he fills to the top as shown in this painting by Biagio d'Antonio and Bartolomeo di Giovanni (Figure 2). A notary sits nearby to record every purchase in a register since the government closely monitors grain sales. (Note: the painting does not show the notary, but then it depicts a biblical episode that is presented in the style of a Renaissance transaction.)

Afraid of famine, Florence's administrators forbade exports, set maximum amounts per person, and fixed the maddeningly volatile price of cereals and bread, day after day (Goldthwaite 1975; Epstein 2000: 157–64; Magni 2015). It wasn't just the sale of cereals that was heavily disciplined. In Renaissance Italy, the market was not a free place: its access was restricted; its operations followed specific times and protocols. In Florence, its management was in the hands of four *camerlenghi*, market supervisors recognizable by their white hats decorated with spikes dipped in red paint (Pecchioli Vigni 1971: 31–32). Other cities relied on other monitoring magistrates, their duties often merging with those of the *sensali*, brokers who performed quality checks, dealing with any disagreement between vendors and customers (Bolognesi 2007; De Luca 2010: 240). Marketgoers knew they had to remain vigilant. The risk of fraud, even small scams, was real. When buying grain, they were advised against filling the measure in one quick pour, which could cause the kernels to settle unevenly and result in pockets of air. Forgetting this, a merchant reports, meant "to lose two or three percent."[1] The painting by Biagio and Bartolomeo gestures to this watchfulness by showing both buyer and measurer intently staring at the latter's hand as it levels the grain.

Preachers contributed to this climate of mistrust. Friar Bernardino of Siena accused merchants of using a smaller *staio* when selling and a larger one when buying.[2] His audience was large – a chronicle reports that the whole city showed up at his sermons (Polecritti 2000: 39–46) – and I sometimes wonder if his popularity led him to exaggerate his words, as if he were trying to inflame more hearts.

---

[1] Paolo da Certaldo, *Libro di buoni costumi*, 43.
[2] Bernardino da Siena, *Prediche volgari*, 2:1117.

**Figure 1** Bushels (*staia*) for grains, sixteenth century. Loggia dei Mercanti, Basilica di San Benedetto, Norcia. Photo: SibilliniWeb.it, around 2013.

**Figure 2** Biagio d'Antonio with the help of Bartolomeo di Giovanni, *The Story of Joseph*, ca. 1487. Detail. Cambridge, UK: Fitzwilliam Museum. Photo: author

**Figure 3** *The Merchant*. In Jacopo da Cessole, *Volgarizzamento del libro de' costumi e degli offizii de' nobili sopra il giuoco degli scacchi*, Florence, 1493

Still, suspicion about standards had grounds. For example, in 1532, an officer in Modena reported that upon inspection of thirty-four *staia*, twenty-two were faulty.[3] In the sixteenth century, Verona unknowingly used various standards of the *piede* (foot) after the city lost its official length, which was not reconstructed until 1696 (Tucci 1974: 307). Even a manual about chess included a rant against the chaos in the marketplace and greedy traders who disregarded the measuring standards on which their sense of the self ought to depend.[4] One of its illustrations (Figure 3) visually argues for their identification.

Skepticism surrounding measurement shaped the attitude of sixteenth-century Florentine historian Vincenzo Borghini. "The nature of weights and measures is both very uncertain and very unstable. They vary from moment to moment, place to place and thing to thing, so much so that to reduce them to a fixed and equivalent term is very difficult, if not impossible."[5] As a way of conclusion, he stated: "neither now nor perhaps at any point have all things been measured in the same way."[6]

---

[3] De' Bianchi, *Cronaca*, 3:382.

[4] Jacopo Da Cessole, *Volgarizzamento*, 86. While Jacopo was a contemporary of Dante, his treatise was reprinted into the late sixteenth century.

[5] Borghini, *Discorsi*, 1:138.     [6] Borghini, *Discorsi*, 1:138.

Most scholars have brushed Borghini's sentiment off as pessimistic. Italian city administrators, after all, took steps to protect and maintain their measurement standards. They had them made in sturdy metals and kept in safes. They displayed standards in public, next to important buildings, to ensure that citizens were aware of them (Lugli 2019a: 65–94). As part of their assigned duties, officers went around town, shop after shop, to check that artisans' tools were accurate. In 1461, the silk guild of Milan requested that all scales be inspected within three days of a sale, thus detaching the purchase from the moment of exchange, which could be reversed were the instruments found imprecise (Santoro 1961: 88–89). Additionally, sellers and buyers developed a complex choreography of sayings, gestures, and regulations not only to guarantee fairness in their transactions but also to instill a sense of fairness (Romano 2015: 110–26). These practices were often reinforced by the decoration of marketplaces and civic buildings with allegories of justice as dependable rulers and monumental inscriptions against fraud (Frojmovič 1996: 35–36; Welch 2005: 79–81). Citizens believed the economic well-being of a city depended on the trust people placed in its ability to maintain order and honesty.

When reading a city's statutes, the governmental initiatives look impressive. Yet Borghini's sense of defeat is understandable given the variety of measurement throughout Italy. Every city employed different standards for different purposes. Land was measured with one unit, wood with another. Silk relied on standards that were separate from those for wool. Venice even developed one weight for gold and one for gold thread (Tucci 1974: 311). There was hardly any relationship between any two standards and, if there was one, it was not always straightforward. In Florence, the length used for measuring fields (*braccio da terra*) was 17/18 the length for cloth (*braccio da panno*). This proportion was awkward because each standard developed independently: Florentine land surveyors had little need to interact with cloth makers. The 17/18 proportion was also a mere simplification: it was first documented in the late fifteenth century when the city government began legislating on both standards and recorded them in a way they found easy to understand. Similarly, Milan's and Turin's "medieval" *piedi* are only known through documents drawn in the sixteenth and seventeenth centuries, respectively (Reguin 2018: 67–68).

Realizing the government's role in shaping the history of measurements exposes the ideology of any dismissal of premodern standards as maddening (Henschel 1855: 9; de Sanctis 1970: 191). This stance assumes the indispensability of a centralized government in managing a growing industry and commerce (Burckhardt 1890: 68–71). It also assumes that humanity's goal is freedom – the freedom to trade, in particular – and portrays state-sponsored standardization as essential to achieve this goal (Scott 1998: 27–36). Little does it matter that this thinking only expresses the ambitions of those who profited from large-scale exchanges. Those who were satisfied with trading locally developed no interest in the measurements they were not using.

The historians who believe that the imposition of standards by governments was necessary for promoting internal homogeneity and global connectivity celebrate the metric system as the greatest achievement. While forced on the French population in the aftermath of the Revolution, it built on ideas developed during the previous two centuries (Tavernor 2007: 70; Crease 2011: 69–98). One significant moment was Flemish engineer Simon Stevin's proposal to base all measurement standards on decimal counting, which would make measuring compatible with mathematical operations. Stevin argued for this change in his 1585 pamphlet *De Thiende* (22–36). Immediately translated into French, *De Thiende* suggested that productivity could be improved by enabling faster computation. A second moment came with Gabriel Mouton's *Observationes* (1670), in which he proposed making the new standard incorruptible by deriving it from the shape of the earth (Alder 2002: 97). From its 1793 introduction to 1960, the meter was described this way, after which it was redefined in terms of wavelengths.

Within two centuries after its debut, almost every country in the world followed France in adopting the meter because it came with closely related standards. (The mass of one liter of water, which is the volume of one cubic decimeter, corresponds to one kilogram.) The domino effect, however, did not happen naturally. Especially at the beginning, it was actively promoted through diplomacy and enforced violently. Napoleon imposed the metric system across his whole empire, including the Italian states, where local governments and intelligentsias welcomed it as a rational replacement for their abstruse standards.

For example, in 1809, citizens of Tuscany adopted the metric system and started thinking of their *braccio da panno* as 583 millimeters.[7] This conversion has never been questioned for two reasons. First, the official standards of the old *braccio* were destroyed when the meter was instituted. (This process of elimination and substitution occurs whenever a new standard is introduced and unfortunately leaves us with only one side of the story.) Second, the metric system has become the gold standard of measurement: it is routinely retouched to meet the latest findings in physics.[8] This care and the trust it engenders have led most historians to view metric conversions as mere technical changes rather than profound cultural transformations (Tucci 1974). When scholars open their studies by reporting that the Florentine *braccio* corresponded to 583

---

[7] *Tavole di riduzione*, 1809: 13–14. The metric law dates to December 19, 1808. See Zangheri 1987.

[8] The last revision took place on May 20, 2019.

millimeters, they ignore that Florentines did not see millimeters.[9] Florentines divided their *braccio* into 20 *soldi* and each *soldo* into 12 *denari*, so most of them ignored anything smaller than one *denaro* – "the little one," as they called it – which can only be approximately rendered as 2.4 millimeters.

When you become aware of how widespread such present-biased distortions are, Borghini's doubts gain traction. In his work, which was published in the same year as Stevin's pamphlet, Borghini asks if we put too much trust in measurement. We tend to think of standards as enduring tools, but they are slippery. As constructions by humans, after all, they are just as flawed. Most historians counter this skepticism; even the most cautious among them accept that past measurements standards can be reconstructed in some form. Not doing so would bring the very project of history to collapse. For what historical picture can anyone offer if measurements, the very means to provide a tangible sense of the past, remain out of reach?

This Element takes seriously the idea that measurements are not self-evident, recognizing that the rationality they express is coextensive with the cultural desires that generated them. As a result, it accepts that many aspects of the Renaissance, just like its measurement standards, are lost to us. This is why I occasionally speak in the first person: it is a reminder that both history writing and measuring involve subjective judgments, even if they often claim to be and are mistaken for absolute truths.

This survey explores objects, practices, and ideas that can help us understand the roles of measurements of fifteenth- and sixteenth-century Italy. Although the topic of quantification is huge, for it is a fundamental aspect of life, this study is deliberately slim. Therefore, the following pages provide only an overview and offer points of comparison for further study on the subject, much like how standards serve as a reference for unknown objects.

This Element, however, is not a random collection of examples; it is organized around two main themes. The first theme is to recognize measurement as a discipline that developed practices and concepts that existed outside and across the fields of knowledge to which it was applied. This approach is unusual because many scholars view measurement as a technique to achieve something else. Architecture historians study geometry as a framework for form and style, economists consider estimates to quantify revenues, and philologists study measuring exercises in manuscripts to construct codicological lineages, not because they think measuring may add anything to their lives. In each case, measurement is often treated cursorily, with its procedures dismissed as elementary and its diagrams given little attention. In contrast, this Element sets out to present measurements as producing a distinct culture. Throughout the fifteenth

---

[9] There are, of course, exceptions like Marina 2006: 545–46.

and sixteenth centuries, many built careers out of its mastery and tried to solve its limitations, eventually developing the standards that we use today.

This is, however, only the Element's secondary theme. For the main one, keep on reading.

## 1.2 The Florentine *Braccio*

An historian, Borghini studied the Florentine nobility and encountered documents that quantified their estates in feet, a puzzling standard since, in his time, fields were measured in *braccia da terra*. Borghini (*Discorsi* 1:85) read in a medieval chronicle that the old foot was named after Liutprand, the king who ruled over parts of Tuscany in the eighth century. (Today, historians debate whether such a standard even existed as they acknowledge Liutprand's reliance on oral arrangements, on which see Chiavari 1981.) Borghini must have known a foot was once displayed on the San Pancrazio gate. Florence's archives preserve nine documents, dating from 1083 to 1207, that define a foot standard this way (Manni 1734: 125–83; Uzielli 1899: 23).

Gateways carrying standards were common in Borghini's day. For incoming merchants, these displays marked the threshold to a distinct trading ground. For the customs officers who spent their days by those barriers, they were the standards by which they quantified imported goods and calculated duties. Only a few portals still preserve them. Volterra's San Francesco gate is incised with the *canna* (Caciagli 1978). Fano's Roman arch carries the outlines of roof tiles and two lengths (Fiorini 2015: 80) (Figure 4). Florence's San Pancrazio gate, however, was demolished three centuries before Borghini was born (Sznura 1975: 70–72). Borghini's source, Giovanni Villani, was the sole chronicler to provide a cursory definition: the foot was "a bit less than the *braccio* we currently employ."[10]

Around the time Villani was writing – that is, 1325 – the foot had fallen into disuse as the Florentine government started relying on the *braccio da panno* of the Arte di Calimala, the guild of merchants who imported cloth from northern Europe (Filippi 1889: 125; Atwell 2006: 195–96). A contract of 1321 for a house sale shows that surveyors used the *braccio*.[11] By turning a corporative standard into the city's standard, the government took advantage of a well-looked-after tool by which Florence was known internationally. Florence was not alone in reshaping its identity around its commercial successes: Italian cities like Verona and Bologna also elevated their most illustrious corporations' tools to the rank of civic standards (Lugli 2019a: 80–87). Such assimilations came about because guilds were enmeshed with civic administrations: their members took on leadership roles and contributed to shaping the

---

[10] Villani, *Nuova Chronica* 3.9.    [11] Manni 1739–86, vol. 21, *giunta* 4, p. 50.

(a)                                                 (b)

**Figure 4** Standards of the roof tile and fragments of two lengths,
Porta Romana, Fano. Photo: author

city's affairs (Molho 1968: 26). In 1323, the Arte di Calimala supplied the city of Florence with a contingent of 200 soldiers (Giuliani 2006: 17–18). It is therefore unsurprising that two years later the Florentine statutes (*Statuto del podestà* 4.32) ordered their *braccio* to be reproduced in "two or three places at least" so citizens could familiarize themselves with it. Today, one of these places is said to be a wall on Via de' Cerchi, a few steps away from Palazzo Vecchio, the town hall (Figure 5). There is no documentation on it, and the display is unique. I never came across an official standard framed by bricks, as is the case here. Official standards tend to be cut in hard stone (like in Assisi, Padua, and Vicenza), not friable clay. I wonder if the tourist attraction may be the repurposed bottom of a one-braccio-wide door or window frame.

After the endorsement by the Florentine government, more artisans are recorded employing the Calimala *braccio*. It became the standard of the Arte della Lana, the guild of wool cloth makers, which employed around one-third of the Florentine workforce and appointed seventy-two measurers alone.[12] Soon after, the *braccio* appears in architectural contracts (Ascani 1997: 150–56). A document from 1357 indicates it was used for the planning of Florence's cathedral (Guasti 1887: 94; Trachtenberg 1997: 295). By the fifteenth century, only land was measured by a different length, the *braccio da terra*, a standard believed to originate from the San Pancrazio foot (Uzielli 1899: 14), even if there is no evidence for it. In his mathematical digest, Luca Pacioli (*Summa*, 1494, f. 6 v) defines it for the first time as 17/18 of the *braccio da panno*. When applied to the *braccio da panno* of 583 millimeters, it produces a *braccio da terra* of about 551 millimeters.

---

[12] *Statuto dell'Arte della lana*, 65. The stats come from Villani, *Nuova Chronica* 12.94.

**Figure 5** Standard of the Florentine *braccio*. Florence, via de'
Cerchi. Photo: author

Here we go again: I am joining the crowd and turning old standards into millimeters, hanging on to values provided by Napoleon's administration. It is a most fallacious operation also because the metric conversions do not relate to the Renaissance tools. Instead, they convert the standards employed after 1782, when Grand Duke Peter Leopold had them retouched in preparation for their introduction across the whole of Tuscany.[13] The revamping fell to the mathematician Leonardo Ximenes (1716–86), who owned a state-of-the-art *toise*, France's main pre-metric length standard, a gift by the mathematician Charles Marie de la Condamine.[14] Ximenes may have had blind faith in his new tool, but his report (*Del Vecchio e nuovo gnomone*, 1–10) offers a bleak picture. He reports that, upon commencing his investigation, he found four lengths that were identified in Florence as the city's official *braccia*, none of which matched another. Ximenes quickly dismissed two – bent, stretched out, probably mislabeled – to focus on the

---

[13] *Tavole di ragguaglio*, 1782. Peter Leopold's edicts are in *Relazioni*: 281 (March 13, 1781, and July 11, 1782). Peter Leopold's process of standardization continued his father's, on which see Guarducci 2009, 143.

[14] The event is recounted in De la Condamine, *Extrait*: 348 and 400.

others, mounted by the entrance of the Bargello palace, one above the other at eye level: the *braccio da panno* and *braccio da terra*. It is important to remark that Ximenes did not measure them in their entirety. Their extremities were eroded, their bodies irregular. He determined their lengths by measuring fractions of each and multiplying them accordingly. He repeated the operation a few times and then averaged out his findings to make the two dimensions correspond to Pacioli's proportion of 17/18. The *braccio da panno*, he concluded, was 258.454 Parisian *lignes*, the *braccio da terra* 244.095.[15]

Now: what monstrous form of quantification is this? Ximenes cobbled together heterogeneous procedures (direct measuring, multiplication, calculation of the mean) and even corrected his findings to satisfy Pacioli's ratio, thus bending a scientific (read: self-sufficient) operation to a pragmatic (that is, political) goal. Measuring should be an open-ended process, a jump in the dark, whose results ought to be accepted for what they are rather than confirm someone's desires. Yet, no one noticed Ximenes's aberrant practice besides the scientists who, following the unification of Italy in 1861, reconverted all of Italy's pre-metric standards (*Tavole di ragguaglio*, 1877, 675–76). When dealing with Tuscany, the members of the Royal Commission for Weights and Measures admitted to being at a loss for, in the absence of dependable, pre-metric standards, they were forced to rely on Ximenes's work. Unfortunately, historians of Tuscany do not acknowledge this problem.

## 1.3 Metaphysics

The standards displayed outdoors were particularly prone to weathering and needed to be replaced regularly. City statutes outlined the procedures for their substitution, which involved high-ranking officers inspecting the stone slabs every few months (usually six) and repairing them if necessary (Guidoni 1989: 376). According to the statutes of Florence (*Statuta populi et communis Florentiae* 4.77), it was the responsibility of the *Capitano del popolo*, the police chief, to examine standards for grain, wine, oil, pulse, and salt within the first month after his appointment. Even if it was assumed that the replacement standard was carefully made, it was still made at a different time and by hand, possibly using different tools, which means that it would not be identical to the original standard. Additionally, each time a standard was replaced, the government did not update the private standards employed by artisans, who continued to use them, believing their tools were equivalent to the matrix even if they were not derived from it.

Slippages also occurred during every use. How much grain does a *staio* actually hold, after all? If you press the grain, you can fit more in. If you mound it, you can fit even more. So how do you ensure a *staio* consistently holds the same amount of

---

[15] In a *toise* there are 864 *lignes*.

grain? To reduce disputes, governments decreased the numbers of measurers as consistency reduces errors. They also devised specific procedures. In Pistoia, measurers hit the *quartino* twice to evenly distribute the kernels, using either their foot or their hand (Rauty 2003: 243). From at least 1325 (*Statuto del podestà* 4.32), measurers also leveled the top of the grain with a scraper called a *rasiera*, but only once. Modena adopted this practice, but, as its results were inconsistent, it began weighing grain in 1530. According to the local chronicler Tommasino De' Bianchi (*Cronaca*, 3:170), this switch caused outrage.

It is difficult to assign change to measurement given that measurement presents itself as unchanging. Most historians assume permanence without question. The most scrupulous among them view standards as a series of good-enough tools, fluctuating around an average or ideal value (Finiello Zervas 1979: 9). However, even this approach stems from the desire that a perfect standard must have existed at some point, which is what governments claimed. I often contemplate the possible sources of this desire, and my reflections often lead me to religion.

Religion played important roles in the history of measurement. Churches often served as places for safekeeping standards, with one notable example being Genoa, which kept its measures in its cathedral from 1184 until the nineteenth century (Rocca 1871: 7–8). Religious orders also provided a pool of skilled measurers, including Friar Pacioli, who wrote a popular treatise on mathematics (Sangster, Stoner, and McCarthy 2008) and Friar Giocondo of Verona (1433–1515), a notable architect in Italy and France. Some of the most influential ideas for the metric system came from clergymen such as French abbot Mouton and Jesuit Tytus Liwiusz Burattini (1617–81), a vocal advocate for international standards who lived in Warsaw (Favaro 1901: 17–19, 108–10; Tancon 2005: 17–18). Ximenes was also a Jesuit.

Besides the attention religious institutions paid to measurement, standards are presented as incorruptible within Christian thinking because only theology is fully invested in eternity. God "disposed all things by measure, number, and weight," states the Book of Wisdom (11:20). Many medieval theologians took this verse as the foundation for their belief that God's creation was ordered mathematically (de Lubac 1959–64: 4:10–13). Saint Augustine (*De genesi ad litteram* 4:3.7) considered measure, number, and weight as qualities with which God identified out of magnanimity – as a way for humans to access him. Many preachers publicized this generosity while reminding their audience that to compare their defective lives to God's perfection was a way to accept their limitations. Dominican friar Girolamo Savonarola spoke of the paradox of "measuring God with the standard of men,"[16] and the preacher Giovanni Nesi, in a sermon from 1478 (*Orationi*, f. 21 r), asked his listeners to think of

---

[16] Savonarola, *Prediche sopra Iob*, f. 395v.

divine love as measureless.[17] This impossibility did not deflate interest in dimensions. On the contrary, it positioned supreme measuring in the heavens, as the philosopher Giovanni Pico della Mirandola (1463–94) pointed out (*La dignità dell'uomo*, 70) when declaring that one should not "confuse divine arithmetic with merchants' accounting."

Ancient texts reassured Renaissance scholars of the divine nature of measurement. They ignored that the Book of Wisdom was written after and influenced by many works of Greek philosophy (Baslez 2005). Humanists did not historicize the Bible, but rather saw the overlaps with classical writing as evidence of the existence of natural truths. (The Venetian scholar Sebastiano Erizzo [1525–85] stated this explicitly in his commentary on Plato's *Phaedo*.)[18] It wasn't just a few ancient authors who spoke of the heavens as the repository of perfect magnitudes. This idea, of Pythagorean origins, was also espoused by Philo, Cassiodorus, and Boethius (Joost-Gaugier 2006: 101–33). In *Timaeus* (35b-5-35c2), Plato describes a demiurge creating the cosmos by doubling, tripling, and quadrupling matter in a series of proportional shifts that presupposes measuring (Gregory 2022). The popular fifteenth-century preacher Roberto Caracciolo (*Spechio de la fede*, f. 34 v) cited *Timaeus* as compatible with so many cosmologies (Cicero's *Dream of Scipio* and his commentary by Macrobius, Jerome's *Commentary on Daniel*, Thomas Aquinas's *Quaestiones*) as to conclude that no one, regardless of their upbringing, could deny "the measure and the ordered shape [*regula*] of all creatures."[19] Even Pico's request to separate huckstering from divine measures ultimately draws from Plato (*Republic* 7.525d), who states that true measurement is fixed and eternal. The divine aspirations of measuring were so strong that metaphysical thinking became the domain of exactness and certitude. "God is absolute precision itself," stated the great mathematician Nicholas of Cusa (1401–64).[20]

Given all of this history, it is not surprising to find that Aristotle discussed measuring in *Metaphysics*. There, he argued for two different forms of quantification. "We call a quantity that which is divisible into constituent parts of which each is by nature a one and a 'this' [more on this 'this' in a second]. A quantity is a multitude if it is numerable, a magnitude if it is measurable" (*Metaphysics* 5.1020a). The second sentence provides the key to understanding the first. Numbers identify discrete entities, such as the quantity of kernels in a sack, which are counted one by one. Their number cannot be questioned, and arithmetic is beyond doubt. Instead, a magnitude is continuous and needs to be

---

[17] The idea returns in other sermons. See Edelheit 2008: 194n, 202n. On Nesi, see Vasoli 1977, 51–128.
[18] Erizzo, *I dialoghi*, 223–24, 233.     [19] On Caracciolo's success, see Mariani 2022: 298–308.
[20] Nicholas of Cusa, *The Layman*, 41.

broken to be quantified. The tool for this rupture is the unit of measure, which Aristotle simply indicates as "this" in the first sentence. Change the dimension associated with "this," Aristotle says, and a new magnitude will follow. Aristotle repeated this point when he defined measure as "that by which quantity is known" (Aristotle, *Metaphysics* 10.1052b20), as did Euclid in his *Elements* (7.2). Geometry, literally the measuring (*-metria*) of the earth (*geo-*), came to be understood as the practice of breaking land into fields.

Aristotle's definition explains why most discussions of measurement coincide with a list of units. Frontinus's *De limitibus*, Isidore of Seville's *Etymologies* (15.15.1–2), Domenico Massaria's 1511 treatise on pharmacological weights (*De Ponderibus*, ff.1 r–11 r), and even Luca Peto's 1573 study of antique standards (*De mensuris*, ff. 2 v–9 r) all agree that measuring is the establishment of a unit – Aristotle's "this." It is only then that geometry can accommodate arithmetical rules. However, these treatises do not mention that the application of a standard is hardly straightforward (Russell 1990; Michell 1997). "Only when they know it in terms of this measure, they [humans] think that they know the quantity," warns Aristotle (*Metaphysics*, 10.1053a1). In 1619, Johannes Kepler repeated the point (*Harmonice Mundi*, 8, def. 7) to define the scope of geometry. However, in doing so, he missed Aristotle's emphasis on subjectivity. Units are not found within magnitudes, but in their perceptions, because magnitudes are continuous and units are projected onto them. Yet, Aristotle notes, when measuring, one behaves "as though someone else measured." This transference, which makes a personal decision pass as an objective experience, constitutes both the aporia of measurement and its source of power.

Aristotle's emphasis on perception explains why Renaissance governments relied on officials when measuring. These figures were given the authority to dictate where a standard started and ended. Since it was impossible to make any tool self-sufficient (again: how much grain does a *staio* actually contain?), the decision rested on trusted people. In a sense, the measurer was a miniature demiurge, reordering the world at every commercial transaction. It is in reference to judicial authority that in Dubrovnik the measure of the city's ell is incised at the feet of a statue of Orlando (Figure 6, on which see Pavlović 2006: 423). Orlando is the knight often taken as a defender of freedom. However, since the late Middle Ages, he was mostly identified as the servant of Charlemagne, Europe's first lawmaker (Pötschke 2002: 177–237). His presence above the standards not only alluded to the safety of Dubrovnik's measurements, guarded by an invincible warrior, but also reminded citizens that measuring was subject to judicial authority.

(a)

(b)

**Figure 6** Standard of *lakat*, 1419. Dubrovnik, Trg Luža, Orlando column.
Photo: Dubravko Lenert

## 1.4 Measurement and the Renaissance

Little of this thinking is overt in Renaissance treatises. Borghini's voice is one of
the very few raised against a wall of unsuspecting celebrations of measurement.
Consider Leon Battista Alberti (*On Sculpture*, 125), who speaks of the "accurate
and constant recording of measurements." Or leaf through Alessandro
Piccolomini's praise of astrologers and geometers (*La sfera del mondo*, 242)
for having found "the measures of celestial bodies ... with most certain
demonstrations." Many teachers, lawmakers, and parents put their faith in
measurement as a truth and a necessity whose benefits were inexhaustible.
Their endorsements reached so far that repetition alone may explain why,
even today, so many historians promote measuring as a venue for progress.
Engineers like Stevin came up with a reform that sped up the application of
arithmetic operations to the measuring of physical artifacts. Scientists like
Galileo aspired to unprecedented levels of precision (Bredekamp 2019: 62,

223–27). The period known as the Renaissance is the antechamber of the palatial structure of modernity, with modernity defined as the effort to remove ambiguity and increase predictability (Beck 2010: 38). Or, rather, the Renaissance is modernity's mason's yard: the area where its structural elements, such as an investment in measuring, were laid down and prepared for use.

The Renaissance is often presented as having developed a unique relationship with measuring. Historians stress that fifteenth-century education placed exceptional value on mathematical skills (Black 2007: 52–54; Saiber 2017), which shaped the ways people saw the world (Baxandall 1972: 100–01; Hendrix 2017). A testament to this interest is the popularity of *libri d'abaco*, math and accounting exercise books that became part of the school curriculum for children from the mid-thirteenth century until the end of the sixteenth (Ulivi 2015). The image of architects carefully recording the dimensions of walls, columns, and cornices on sheets of paper is often associated with this period (Figures 8 and 21). A writer emphasizes the ubiquitousness of table clocks as a historical watershed (Crosby 1988: 80). Another mentions how improved measuring instruments fueled engineering, land transport, and international trade (Cox 2016: 82). The list continues to include agronomy, hydraulics, and any other princely interest (Barker 2022).

The belief in a greater engagement with measurement during the Renaissance is largely due to the increased availability of printed books and archival material, which makes it easier to find references to measurement. However, this argument is flawed because it relies on a change in the type of evidence used to support it. It also ignores the history of measurement, as standards did not change between the Middle Ages and the Renaissance. Their management and precision hardly shifted. Some cities adopted the standards of other cities due to intense trading, such as Pisa appropriating the Florentine standards (Chiarini, *Libro*, f. 45 r), but these are just cases of musical chairs. The content of geometry and accounting publications is similar to those produced two centuries earlier. Military historians consider the mathematization of artillery trajectories put forward by Niccolò Tartaglia in his *Nova Scientia* (1537) more aspirational than transformational of warfare (Black 2005: 51–52). Even the innovations often attributed to the Renaissance, such as perspective and the concept of the "life-size," are modifications of earlier ideas, as will be discussed later. The discovery of a standard for the ancient Roman foot, which was celebrated as a major achievement, actually highlighted the inadequacies of the Renaissance in terms of measurement.[21]

This is perhaps what intrigues me about the routine pairing of measuring and the Renaissance. It is not that a shift in measurement practices defined the

---

[21] I here follow the historian Jacques Le Goff (2015: 79–112), who proposed the Renaissance should be dissolved into the "long Middle Ages," a period stretching until the eighteenth century and defined by monarchical reliance on agriculture, feudal bonds, disinterest in secularization, and classicist revivals, including the Renaissance.

Renaissance. What I see is the reverse operation: people who believe the Renaissance existed – students who have been taught to care for it – hang its existence onto measuring. They do even if told the Renaissance is a myth, a term coined in the nineteenth century (Ruggiero 2015: 205–07), because they also learn to appreciate quantification as a marker of stability. Measuring, Aristotle reminds us, removes events from the fallibility of subjective experience. To rely on something this sturdy brings comfort.

Yet, as this Element stresses, measuring is deceptive. In the process of transforming an object into a magnitude, a measurer must ignore some of the object's characteristics. To measure a piece of fabric, early modern cloth sellers compared it to a sturdy rod (Figure 7). To agree that the product was one *braccio* long, they overlooked the fabric's elasticity and took its frayed borders as if they were clean-cut. They also assumed that their tools were perfect replicas of the official standard. I could add more details, but the point is clear: as the production of any dimension is an estimate, it prioritizes some features over others,

**Figure 7** A tailor's shop. In *Tacuinum Sanitatis*, early fifteenth century. Paris, Bibliothèque Nationale de France, Département des manuscrits, NAL 1673, fol. 95r

thus paving the way for operations that would not have been possible had the original complexity been maintained.

In particular, measuring requires the elimination of any aspect that may question the process itself. I am trying to pick my words carefully here: "to eliminate" means to keep something outside (*ex-*) of a limit. Measuring can be seen as a form of enclosure, the first step in transforming land and even water into resources from which to produce commodities. By marking a limit, measuring emerges as an exclusionary activity, the modus operandi of a binary logic that separates what can be owned from what cannot. It is perhaps not surprising that some scholars have wondered if the Renaissance ought to coincide with the rediscovery not of antiquity but of the *Corpus Agrimensorum Romanorum*, an anthology of ancient Roman treatises on land division (Toneatto 1994–95: 2, 547–54). These books (including Frontinus's *De limitibus*, which we have already encountered) did not simply teach measuring techniques and how to solve boundary disputes, but also revived the ethos of the Roman Empire for seizing land (Cuomo 2000). Measuring is not just a mental exercise involving imaginary lines but part of a violent process of exerting control over territory by depriving their owners and physically transforming it through actions such as digging ditches and laying roads.

During the Renaissance, the selective manipulation of land and material that is necessarily a result of measuring sustained a particular ambition to remake the world anew. This is how measuring came to support the Renaissance: not as a tool capable of recording reality, but as providing a psychological state of being in control whose self-deception was not registered by those who benefited from it. Exploring this creative dimension of measurement is the main goal of this Element, as anticipated.

I recognize this creativity in three main processes, strategies through which fifteenth- and sixteenth-century disciplines that embraced measurement constructed their specific interpretations and visions of reality. They serve as titles for the following sections. The first, "Elimination of Time" (Section 2), looks at the effects produced by thinking that the dimensions of buildings and objects do not change over the centuries. It focuses on archaeology and antiquarianism, two forms of retrieval of the past that encouraged the recording of dimensions and shaped architectural and even legal practices. Section 3, "Elimination of Matter," deals with pictorial perspective, fencing, and tailoring, activities that promoted the idea that the physical world was best understood through its outlines. By showing measurers' disinterest in material concerns, this section reflects on the consequences of hylomorphism. Finally, Section 4, "Elimination of Interpretation," pays attention to the many efforts to turn measuring into a self-evident practice, one that excludes the interpreter and thus passes measuring as self-sufficient and universal. By exploring these overlooked processes of Renaissance measuring, which faded toward the end of the sixteenth century, I hope this Element may generate intriguing perspectives on early modern Italian and European culture while inviting you to explore measurement as a process with its own concepts, tensions, and history.

## 2 Elimination of Time

### 2.1 Measuring, Reading

The Renaissance is often presented as a shift in the attention bestowed on books and what they said. For the elite tastemakers called "humanists," the possibility of reviving the past arose from a new engagement with texts. In Pliny (36.15 and 17), the humanist Ciriaco d'Ancona (1391–1452) encountered descriptions of monuments that emphasized their dimensions, including the height of obelisks, the extension of labyrinths, and the circumference of the Sphinx's head (Fane-Saunders 2016: 238–40). Those specifications shaped his mode of viewing ancient architecture, and, when he visited the Parthenon in Athens, Ciriaco also measured the diameter of its columns and the length of its ceiling beams.[22] Similarly, Vitruvius's ancient treatise of architecture prompted its readers to consider buildings from a builder's perspective: What was the size of a hall? How long should a portico be? How much weight does limestone lose after boiling?[23] While Vitruvius's manual was widely copied during the Middle Ages (Herselle Krinsky 1967; Verbaal 2016: 218–20), it was considered essential by the humanist Pier Candido Decembrio, who disseminated it among the Italian aristocracy starting in the 1440s (Ciapponi 1960: 88–91; Clarke 2002: 322–24).

Quantification is a common rhetorical strategy when discussing large buildings and structures (Stewart 1993: 71). Writers break these massive edifices into smaller components that can be described more easily and whose fragmentary nature suggests the existence of something bigger. Measuring contributes to this process by expressing a building's dimensions in numerical form, allowing it to be abstracted from the physical structure itself and yet somewhat standing for it. For instance, Poggio Bracciolini (1380–1459) believed it was sufficient to describe Roman aqueducts by recording their lengths.[24] Little does it matter that he did not measure them directly but transcribed their dimensions from

---

[22] Cyriac of Ancona, *Later Travels*, 17–21.    [23] Vitruvius 2.5.3.
[24] Bracciolini, *De Varietate Fortunae*, 237–38.

Frontinus's report on ancient water management (*De aquaeductu Urbis Romae*, 31), which he had discovered in a monastery (Rubinstein 1958).

Humanists did not simply imitate past architectural ekphrases. They used measurement to engage with the world they encountered in written accounts and wished to translate it into their own time (Mazzocco 1982: 183–95). Bracciolini embarked on a journey through Rome around 1444 (the year Ciriaco wrote about the Parthenon), during which he not only gazed at the aqueducts stretching out into the distance, but also carefully examined the remains of once-grand buildings and the roads overgrown with vines and covered in manure. Even though he could only imagine their former splendor, he was able to measure what remained, trusting in the ability of measurement to transcend time (Bracciolini, *De varietate fortunae*, 243). He therefore paced the perimeter of the city walls and the Praetorian barracks "most diligently" (*diligentissime*), a term that held significant emotional weight for humanists. To read the orations of past authors and copy their letters "most diligently" was not only to engage with their work in an admiring, meticulous manner, but also to do so with one's body.[25] To physically retrace the circuit of ancient Rome, step by step, was the physical equivalent of transcribing every word of Seneca's letter by hand, a way to go through a past achievement as if recreating it piece by piece.

Measuring ancient Roman monuments often involved physically climbing them, as depicted in the unique drawing shown in Figure 8, where a person ascends the ruins of the Forum of Nerva. He did so to measure its trabeation, which was then reproduced on the other side of the sheet as if it were at eye level (Scaglia 1991). Like book copying – which also required extensive travel, often to remote monastery libraries – measuring involved seeking out close contact with an object. This proximity was a form of dwelling sustained by the belief that studying something thoroughly is a way of remaking it, collapsing the viewer's time into that of the original artist.

Petrarch (1304–74) and Giovanni Dondi (1330–88), often credited with inaugurating the Renaissance, provide a historical example of the overlap between transcribing and measuring. Petrarch is considered the grandfather of literary studies for his efforts to search for complete ancient texts and thoroughly engage with them (Mazzotta 1993: 24). His project was shared by his physician Dondi, famous for a letter that came to represent humanists' awe for classical monuments (Panofsky 1960: 208–10; Barkan 1999: 47–49) and the first metrological description of Rome. Known as *Iter Romanum*, the text drops the reader in front of St. Peter's obelisk, which "measures around eight

---

[25] An example should suffice: "Cum eloquentiae studiosissimus sis et oratorum nostrorum scripta diligentissime legas et avidissime perscruteris" (cit. in Accame Lanzillota 1986: 99).

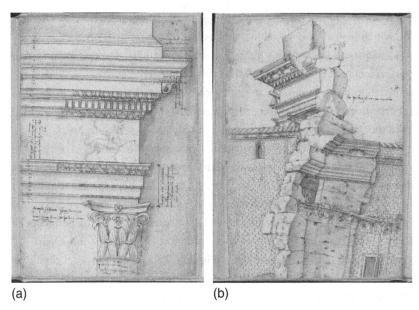

(a)                    (b)

**Figure 8** Pseudo-Cronaca. The cornice of the Forum of Nerva
and a measurer climbing it. Florence, Biblioteca Nazionale Centrale, Fondo
Nazionale II.I.429, ff. 50r-v

feet per side at the base and is approximately 60-foot tall, or ten *perticae*. However, a priest who lives nearby said that he had its shadow measured and found it to be 45 *braccia*. And in his chronicle, Martin [of Opawy] wrote that it was one-hundred-twenty feet, as did Eutropius."[26] Dondi's reliance on measurement is said to mark a shift in the evaluation of monuments (Weiss 1988: 53).

Unfortunately, the *Iter* was not written by Dondi (Perucchi 2016). Dondi simply transcribed a specimen of the *Mirabilia Urbis Romae*, descriptions of Rome that often included the dimensions of its buildings (Nichols 1986: 35, 93; Nardella 1997: 168, 174). This was later bound with Dondi's correspondence into a volume, now held in Venice, and mistaken as representing his oeuvre. The attribution error illustrates the confirmation biases produced by periodization and serves as a reminder that it was during the Middle Ages, rather than the Renaissance, that measurements became popularized. City governments displayed standards in public spaces and trumpeted protocols requiring their protection (Lugli 2019a: 65–74).

Those protocols make clear that measuring, at its core, involves comparison: any unknown tool can be validated only by an authoritative standard.

---

[26] Dondi, *Iter Romanum*, 68.

This act is also central to the practice of philology. Angelo Poliziano, one of the most meticulous philologists of the fifteenth century, explains in his *Miscellanea* that a text is authenticated by comparing it to a reliable source (Castano Musicò 1990: 181; Timpanaro 2005: 45–50). Measuring and textual criticism therefore share this fundamental operation. Humanists did not learn about measuring from Pliny, Vitruvius, or Frontinus, but their engagement with their texts validated a comparative mode of thinking in which measuring also participated.[27]

The connection of measuring and philology is made patent by Baldesar Castiglione and Raphael's plan for the restoration of ancient Rome (Quondam 2021: 73–152). In a two-part letter addressed to Pope Leo X (ca. 1519), they proposed classical Rome could be revived by measuring its monuments and reintegrating them using ancient descriptions. They presented reading and measuring as mutually dependent activities: books helped identify monuments, whose extant dimensions confirmed their descriptions. (Di Teodoro 1994: 115–27; Barkan 1999: 40–41).

Castiglione and Raphael's letter reflects a faith in measuring cultivated over a century of surveys and reflections on ancient architectural production (Brothers 2021; Nesselrath 2022). They mention measuring more than thirty times, presenting it as yielding information that is both comparable and complementary to that found in texts. However, their letter also exposes the temporal paradox of measurement. On the one hand, measuring reveals buildings as historical products. By retrieving a building's proportions, architects can determine when it was erected. For example, Castiglione and Raphael describe Rome's postclassical architecture (what they refer as the "Rome of the Barbarians") as having "no measure," while Gothic architecture had regularized proportions but ignored "the proportion of the man and the woman," as prescribed by Vitruvius. Bracciolini had already demonstrated that measuring helped him understand the complex chronology of Rome's city walls, whose dimensional shifts revealed multiple building phases joined together. On the other hand, measuring also allows for the creation of an ideal in which time is suspended. Like philology, which promotes the removal of any spurious element from a text to produce a purified version that is considered original (even if such an original never existed), so measuring offers "principles" (Castiglione and Raphael's word) for restoring any building to a new form that is considered a restoration.

These exciting ideas were not left unexplored. Marcantonio Michiel (1484–1552), a Venetian nobleman living in Rome, wrote that before his death in 1520,

---

[27] See also Smith 1992: 171–98.

Raphael had left sketches of the "original" appearances of ancient Roman ruins (Shearman 2003: 1, 581–82). Collaborators of Raphael continued his ambitious project by publishing descriptions and reconstructions of ancient Rome (Stinger 1985: 67). In 1551, Leonardo Bufalini created a map that was larger than a man with outstretched arms and aimed to restore Roman buildings to their sizes and "locations, fulfilling" measurement's ability to bring the past back to life (Maier 2015: 77–116). Given the idealistic nature of both measuring and philology, it is perhaps not surprising that all these reconstructions remained on paper. However, Castiglione, Raphael, Bufalini, and other antiquarians were not just dealing in dreams. Their delusional optimism was rooted in a discovery: the unearthing of an ancient Roman standard, which finally provided a key for decoding the texts of the past (Mangani 2018: 96–99).

## 2.2 Searching for the Ancient Roman Foot

At the time of Bracciolini's journey through Rome, the humanist Flavio Biondo (1392–1463) expressed his frustrations when working with ancient measurement. While studying the *Antonine Itinerary*, a third-century inventory of the distances between stations along Roman roads, he lamented that he could not understand anything "because our measurement standards are very different from those of the ancients."[28] And not knowing the size of ancient standards, not even the Roman foot, on which the mile depended (since a mile is 1,000 paces or 5,000 feet), meant the distances provided by the *Antonine Itinerary* remained meaningless.[29]

Biondo understood the impossibility of what people sought in books. How could they experience the past if they couldn't even grasp the basic modules of ancient life? Even the most renowned humanists like Bartolomeo Fonzio (1446–1513) or Poliziano couldn't determine the length of the Roman foot. When tasked to define it, they simply repeated that it was equal to twelve *unciae* (inches) or sixteen fingers but provided no actual measurement.[30] The ancient milestones scattered across the Roman countryside offered a potential solution, but none had the means to accurately measure the distance between them (Rowland 1998: 136).

In his treatise *De Asse* (1515), French humanist Guillaume Budé sought to provide concrete evidence for the abstract definitions of ancient measurements. He studied the ancient coins in aristocratic collections, weighing them himself "with a diligence, I believe, worthy of ancient bankers."[31] He used portable

---

[28] Biondo, *De Roma Instaurata*, f. 1r. On the history of this publication, see Muecke 2017: 625–35.
[29] Isidore of Seville, *Etymologies*, 15.16.2.
[30] Poliziano, *Epistle to Franciotto Orsini*; Fonzio, *Letters to Friends*, 148–54.
[31] Budé, *De Asse*, 261.

**Figure 9** Marinus van Reymerswaele (attr.), *The Banker and His Wife.*
Valenciennes, Musée des Beaux Arts, P.46.1.47. Detail. Photo: RMN-Grand
Palais / René Gabriel Ojéda

scales like those depicted in Figure 9 in order to ensure consistency in his
measurements (Yamey 1989: 47–56). Measuring may be subjective, but using
the same tool can produce more accurate results.

Thanks to his scales, Budé noticed shifts in the weight of the *aureus*, the
Roman gold coin, and was able to develop an understanding of metallic purity,
ancient salaries, and even inflation (Gadoffre 1997: 262–65). However, he was
unable to repeat the same feat for linear standards. Instead, he turned to Pliny
(15.26), who described the pods of the carob trees as one *uncia* thick. Budé
knew six carob seeds weighed one *scripulus*, or a gram, and thus used the plant
as a kind of botanical standard for ancient lengths and weights (Eran 1986: 248–
61; Carlà 2009: 68–70).[32] He then mistakenly concluded that the ancient Roman
foot corresponded to the modern Parisian foot (Delaruelle 1907: 150–51).[33]

Budé must have been disappointed to find out that around the time his magnum
opus was being published, a lawyer from Vicenza, Leonardo Porzio, issued a slim
book (*De sestertio, pecuniis, ponderibus et mensuris antiquis*, 1514) in which he
included the length of the Roman foot (Figure 10). Porzio had found the standard

---

[32] Budé, *De Asse*, 20.
[33] Budé's error was perhaps confirmation bias since he was convinced that the "Gallic spirit" was the
most suitable to classical studies (*De Asse*, 7–9). On Budé's nationalism, see McNeil 1975: 28.

(a)

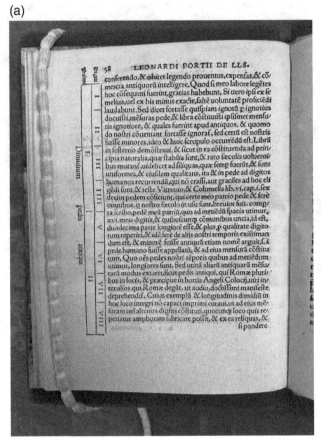

(b)

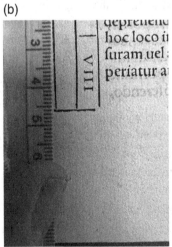

**Figure 10** Roman Foot. Leonardo Porzio, *De sestertio, pecuniis, ponderibus et mensuris antiquis,* 1520 (1st ed. 1514). Special Collections, Green Library, Stanford University. Photo: author

**Figure 11** Funerary altar of Cossutius Claudus and Cossutia Arescusa, first century CE. Rome, Musei Capitolini, Palazzo Nuovo: S 215. Photo: Archivio fotografico dei Musei Capitolini © Roma, Soprintendenza Capitolina ai Beni Culturali

carved on the cinerary altar of the ancient builder Cossutius Claudus (Figure 11), which was then owned by the antiquarian Angelo Colocci (La Rocca and Parisi Presicce 2010, cat. 15).[34] While Porzio does not comment on the significance of this discovery, its momentousness is indicated by the fact that the 293 mm foot (or, more accurately, its half since Porzio had to fit it on the page) was the only illustration in the book.

Colocci accumulated an impressive number of ancient measurements and treatises on them (Rowland 1998, 118–39). Amongst his most prized possessions were a bronze *sextarius* (a pint-sized standard of capacity) and a *congius* (a volume six times the *sextarius*), whose inscription "by the exact measure from the Capitol" (*Mensurae exactae in capitolio*) identified it as Rome's official standard (Gasparotto 1996: 296–97). Romans kept their measurements by the temple of Jupiter Maximus (Guarducci 1983: 153–56), a function the

---

[34] On Porzio and Colocci's encounter, see Ubaldini, *Vita*: 283–84.

Capitoline hill retained during the Middle Ages (Maetzke 1990: 98) and the Renaissance.[35]

Colocci's collection was well known. As papal secretary, he was at the center of a powerful network of humanists, collectors, and artists such as Raphael. Many European publications – from scholarly works to guidebooks – recommended visiting his collection to see the Roman foot.[36] Their praise reflects the enthusiasm for finally solving this long-lasting problem (Günther 1981/82). Colocci's own relief is evident in the notes he took for a treatise on ancient measurement, although he never completed it. Those notes paint a picture of Rome as a city grateful to those who kept their eyes open for such discoveries. A barber's shop by the Porch of Octavia displayed another Roman foot. An inscription on top of a ten-foot column near the Lateran advertised its height. Colocci wrote that standards could be found in all sorts of places, including tailors' shops, which unsuspectingly used the smooth sacral weights of the ancients as ironing boards (Lattès 1972: 105–06).

Such easiness clashes with studies that suggest Colocci's discoveries were the result of hard work: he purchased properties throughout Rome with the specific purpose of excavating them (Fanelli 1979). Additionally, while Colocci's collection must have been impressive, it was dispersed with the city's sack of 1527 (Bernardi 2017). The plundering left the city in ruins and the remaining artifacts found new owners. According to the French architect Philippe de l'Orme (1514–70),[37] Cossutius's monument passed to the hands of Cardinal Nicola Gaddi. Francesco de Marchi, a Bolognese general working on fortifications for the State of the Church, did not even know of its existence and wrote in his diary (entry of 1535) that architects derived the Roman foot from a nine-foot porphyry column in the church of Santi Apostoli.[38] De Marchi drew its length (340 mm) on the page, unaware it corresponded to the Greek foot, as some suspected.[39]

Perhaps the sack was both prelude and aftermath as it exposed the gatekeeping of early modern Rome. It does not matter how widely it was advertised, Colocci's collection was accessible to only a few. Georg Agricola, a Saxon physician (1494–1555), was unable to access it during the three years he spent in Italy (1523–26). He expressed his disappointment in a treatise (*De mensuris & ponderibus Romanorum atque Graecorum* 1550, 216) that became the

---

[35] In the 1530s, Philippe de l'Orme went to the capital to measure the modern Roman palm as he describes in *Le Premier tome*, f. 131v.

[36] Jacopo Mazzocchi, *Epigrammata* (1521), f. 100v; Mariangelo Accursio, *Diatribae* (1524), f. 85v; Andrea Fulvio, *Antiquitates Urbis* (1527), f. 35r.

[37] De l'Orme, *Le Premier tome*, f. 131v.

[38] Biblioteca Nazionale Centrale, Firenze, Ms Palatino II.I.278, f. 15a.

[39] The observation of the Greek foot comes from Luigi Marini in his edition of de Marchi's *Architettura Militare*: 1, 122.

reference text on ancient measurement in the second half of the century.[40] Agricola's success was well deserved, as his work provided the most comprehensive collation of information, drawing from both contemporary writers and classical sources. He presented his erudition in concise, terse sentences that do not shy away from pointing out errors (such as Poliziano's definition of the sextarius). Agricola's book was particularly useful for deciphering the opaque terminology of pharmaceutical recipes and for its pragmatism, as when Agrippa recognizes a difference between weighing wet and dry ingredients (Pastorino 2021: 127–28). By criticizing both charlatans and lazy scholars, Agricola also emphasized that metrology had a lot of room for improvement.[41]

In 1542, another cinerary urn resurfaced. The pope acquired it and displayed it in the Belvedere, along with his most prized antiquities.[42] The urn belonged to the ancient architect Titus Statilius Aper, depicted on the front with his son and a wounded wild boar (*aper* in Latin). The sides of the urn show surveying and measuring tools, including a Roman foot. This instrument in particular garnered a lot of interest due to its crisp carving, which showed its divisions marked in four palms and sixteen *digiti* (Casamassima and Rubinstein 1993: 75–76). A friend of Budé, the architect Guillaume Philandrier (1505–63) celebrated it in his commentary to Vitruvius (1544), where he describes antiquarians in Rome as divided over the authority of three standards: Colocci's, Statilius's, and the Santi Apostoli porphyry column.[43]

In the 1560s – the precise year is unknown – eight antiquarians (including the Spanish bishop and collector Antonio Agustín) gathered to determine the most reliable foot. They concluded it was Statilius's after verifying it matched the side of a *quadrantal*, a cubic-foot standard of capacity.[44] However, it seems few people were aware of this study. In 1567, the architect Pirro Ligorio (1512–83), a friend of Agustín, mentioned seven feet in private collections, although his reliability has been called into question (Vagenheim 2011).[45] A few years later, the Roman magistrate Luca Peto (1512–81) installed a marble slab with the

---

[40] Copies of Agricola's treatise commented on by eminent scholars survive. Ulisse Aldrovandi's copy is in Bologna (Biblioteca Universitaria A.M.15); Heinrich Glarean's is in Munich (W 2 H. aux 420 #2), on which see Engammare 2013: 105–08. Beatus Rhenanus's is in Sélestat (Bibliothèque Humaniste K 915s Incunables). I'm thankful to Damiano Acciarino for this observation.

[41] Agricola's sentiment was shared by the great humanist Erasmus of Rotterdam, who encouraged him in a letter (number 2529, in Erasmus, *The Correspondence*, 143).

[42] Ulisse Aldrovandi saw it in the Belvedere in 1550 while compiling a list of all of Rome's ancient sculptures. His catalog was published in Mauro's *Le antichità*. Statilius's urn is mentioned at page 122.

[43] Philandrier, *Annotationes*, 98. Generally, see Lemerle 1994: 518.

[44] Chacon, *Toletani Opuscula*, 188–89. I am grateful to William Stenhouse for pointing me to this source. On Chacon's Roman years, see Ruiz 1976.

[45] Biblioteca Nazionale di Napoli, Fondo Farnese XIII.B.4, f. 57r. See Pafumi 2011: ix–xi.

ancient foot and the city's modern length standards in the courtyard of the
Palazzo dei Conservatori on the Capitoline hill.[46] In an accompanying report,
Peto explains he used Colocci's standard as a model because it matched three
metal feet from private collections.

Many studies claim Peto did so in 1535, but it is not possible as he was
a twenty-three-year-old student of law in Bologna at the time (Del Re 1986).
Peto must have commissioned the slab at the time of his report in 1573. After all,
the first erroneous mention of 1535 occurs in the Napoleonic report about the
replacement of Peto's *tabula* with the meter (Scarpellini 1811: 29–30). At six
feet by one (Fedreghini 1752: 39), the slab may have looked like the bottom of
the measurement plaque in Rimini (Figure 12), installed in 1544 to signal the
order the pope brought to the city after defeating the Malatesta family, which
claimed Rimini as their fief.

Although Rome's government approved Peto's standards, doubts about the
ancient Roman foot persisted. Agustín's secretary Jean Matal claims Colocci
confessed, before his death in 1549, that he no longer thought his foot was the
most accurate.[47] Peto lamented that he could no longer find and therefore verify
the Santi Apostoli porphyry column he had seen in his youth. Confusingly, new
treatises were published even though they contained outdated information. In
1599, twenty years after returning to Spain, the Jesuit Juan de Mariana (1536–
1624) published *De Ponderibus et Mensuris*, which made no mention of Peto'
slab and presented as current the metrological landscape of fifty years earlier.

**Figure 12** Rimini Standards (Tavola delle misure), 1544. Palazzo dell'
Arengo, Rimini. Photo: Renato Morselli

---

[46] Peto, *De mensuris et ponderibus*, 11.
[47] Biblioteca Apostolica Vaticana: Vat. Lat. 6039, f. 67r. See Stenhouse 2005, 62.

Initially, I believed this confusion was due to a lack of standardization in communication. However, as I write, I am now considering the possibility that the chaos stemmed from the unique fact that the ancient Roman foot was the first standard without a presiding authority. With no one in charge, debates about the ancient length were able to occurred all over Europe, providing an unlikely testing ground for the development of standards that were not tied to any specific ruler.

## 2.3 Floods

Most of those involved in retrieving ancient standards (Budé, Porzio, Agustín, Matal) were jurists, which prompts questions about the role of law schools in the history of measurement. And the moment one pays attention, evidence pops up everywhere. Porzio's and Budé's treatises were frequently reprinted (Porzio: 1514, 1520, 1524, and 1547; Budé: over seven editions between 1515 and 1541) because every year new students needed textbooks to learn about the standards of the past (Mattone and Olivari 2009: 218–20; Burnett 2017). Students also asked for translations and abridgments (Gueudet 1968; McNeil 1975: 29–31; Davies 1985), fueling a more dynamic market than previously believed. The first printed edition of the *Corpus Agrimensorum Romanorum* (1554) was intended not just for antiquarians but also for lawyers, who commented on it extensively.[48]

Lawyers encountered ancient measurements in the *Corpus Iuris Civilis* (*Body of Civil Law*), the sixth-century legal code that remained foundational 1,000 years later throughout Europe (Rowan 1984; Grendler 2004: 434–36). One of its laws (*Novellae* 334–35) stipulates the proper distance between buildings in ancient Roman feet. Budé began his treatise by discussing the "Si mensor" law of the Corpus (*Digest* 11.6), which pertains to the landowner's rights in a sale where the surveyor is found negligent. Law students would have struggled without any knowledge of ancient measurement.

After graduating as jurisconsults, many ex-students went on to work as *podestà*, or governors in charge of a city's standards.[49] It was the *podestà* who appointed magistrates responsible for resolving local controversies about weights and measures.[50] Measuring required a judicial decision because it was a form of judgment. As it was hard to determine the precise end of a standard (Figure 10b), discrepancies were resolved by an authority determining how to

---

[48] For instance, see Hotman, *De legibus*, 46; Duprat, *Lexicon*, 615.

[49] Consider the Lamborizio family, whose members studied law and became *podestà* of Genova (Giovanni Francesco), Pontremoli (Giovanni Angelo), and Piacenza (Guglielmo). See Valle 1855, 4:423–24.

[50] For an explicit example, see *Ordini e decreti da osservarsi in Bardi e Compiano* (1599), 4–6.

address the issue. The preacher Cornelio Musso (1511–74) emphasized that being "just," a quality of a judge, meant respecting measurement (*Il primo libro*, 169–70).

The story of premodern standards is less about the search for dimensions and more about the struggle to control them at both the micro and macro levels. In 1540, King Francis I of France (1494–1547) removed weights and measures from the jurisdiction of local seigneurs and declared he would standardize all measures in his kingdom. Yet, despite various efforts, Francis and his successors faced strong opposition from local authorities, and it was not until the French Revolution that France established a national measurement system (Kula 1986: 167–83; Cazals 2008: n87). A key element of Francis I's nationalistic project was the hiring of the Milanese Andrea Alciato (1492–1550), who is believed to represent the new humanistic jurist (Kelly 1988: 92) due to his involvement in both historical questions – he published on Tacitus – and technical matters – he wrote a treatise on measurement (*Libellus de veterum ponderibus et mensuris*, 1530). His student François Connan (1508–51) continued this approach and demonstrated, in his influential commentary on the *Corpus Iuris Civilis*, the importance of knowing how to calculate loans, verify wine standards, and, especially, measure fields after a flood (Ducos 2002: 306).[51]

Floods and measuring have been linked since the Egyptians invented geometry to return their fields to their original size after the inundations of the Nile. This origin story was recounted by the ancient authors Herodotus, Frontinus, and Varro (Heilbron 2000: 1–3), but their association reached new heights with Bartolo of Sassoferrato's *Tyberiades*, a treatise entirely dedicated to the topic (Cavallar 2004: 50–51).

Written in 1355 and first printed in Venice in 1472 (Panzanelli Frantoni 2020), Bartolo's treatise addresses questions of land division caused by a river that constantly changes its course, such as who owns alluvial deposits or an island that emerges in the middle of the water. To solve these and other issues, Bartolo turns to geometry (Elden 2013: 228–29). Figure 13, one of his first case studies, shows a shore with an area labeled "alluvio," indicating river deposits that have increased the fields owned by Lucius, Titius, and Caius. Because the river course is now perpendicular to the boundaries separating the fields, Bartolo explains, most jurists would be tempted to extend the boundaries along straight lines into the water. However, this would not be fair as the deposits have not accumulated uniformly: Lucius's field grew twice as much as Caius's. As a solution, Bartolo suggests taking the bottom alluvial line as

---

[51] Connan, *Commentarii*, 7.1.4–5 (pp. 647–50), 7.10 (pp. 744–50), and 3.5 (pp. 237–43).

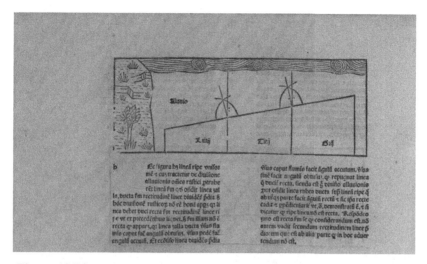

**Figure 13** Diagram. In Bartolo da Sassoferrato, *Tractatus Tyberiadis seu de fluminibus*, Rome: Georg Herolt und Sixtus Riessinger, 1483, f. 7v. Munich: Bavarian State Library, 2 Inc.s.a.169

a reference and prolonging the field sides perpendicularly to it, as indicated by the compass marks in the figure.

Unlike the Egyptians, Bartolo did not use geometry to restore the fields to their original shapes. Instead, his command of geometry – he accurately instructs how to construct the alluvial line when the river bends into an arc or wiggles – served to make time inconsequential rather than erase it. Measuring, which one of Bartolo's commentators described as "certain, infallible, and eternal," instilled the hope that humans no longer had to accept the changes brought about by time.[52]

Bartolo's application of geometrical principles to water had a ripple effect. A notable example can be found in the Roman plaques that record the levels reached by the Tiber during its many floods. As Bartolo knew, Rome was notoriously vulnerable to inundations, so popes had inscriptions installed on Santa Maria sopra Minerva (Figure 14), Sant'Angelo, and the Ripa Grande customs house to allow viewers to visualize invisible water levels above their heads. Placed side by side, the plaques invited comparisons, as demonstrated also by the *avvisi* (news bulletins), one of which stated that the 1557 flood came "within a palm of the sign reached by the [great flood of] 1530."[53] Pope Alexander VII (1599–1667) even had all the disasters of the previous two

---

[52] Bartolo, *La tiberiade*, ed. Claudio Tobalduzi, 54 and 60.
[53] Biblioteca Apostolica Vaticana, Urb. lat. 1038, part A, ff. 265r. See Long 2018: 19–20.

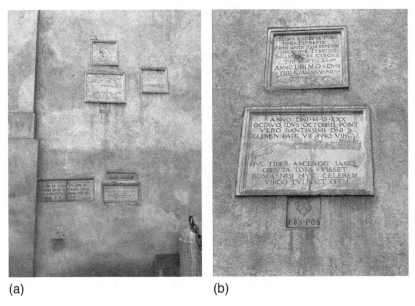

(a)                                           (b)

**Figure 14** Flood markers, sixteenth century. Façade of Santa Maria sopra
Minerva, Rome. Photo: author

centuries juxtaposed in a time-warping diagram (D'Onofrio 1968: 27). While
these plaques abstracted past deluges into lines, they also provided a form of
psychological comfort by reminding people of the tools available for recording
disasters, and, paradoxically, encouraged a certain lack of concern about them
as if measuring floods were a way to control them (Salvestrini 2010: 255–56).

## 2.4 Disparate Standards

When the architect Donato Bramante (1444–1514) traveled to Rome "in a short
amount of time he measured [*misurò*] all the buildings in Rome and its countryside. He did the same as far as Naples and knew every site where there were
ancient things. He measured [*misurò*] what was at Tivoli and Hadrian's villa
and, as will be said at the convenient time, made great use of his findings."

These words are from the 1568 edition of Giorgio Vasari's *Vite* (4:154), more
than half a century after Bramante's death. His account of scrupulousness was
not original: Vasari based it on the description Antonio Manetti (1423–97) gave
of the journey to Rome of Brunelleschi, one of Bramante's role models.[54]
Brunelleschi, Manetti specified, went to Rome in 1400 with Donatello

---

[54] Vasari (*Vite*, 4:145) opens Bramante's biography by saying that he "followed in Brunelleschi's
footsteps."

(surveying requires two people, both scrupulously checking an end of a long distance). The two sketched "almost all of the buildings, and many surrounding places, with dimensions of depth, widths, and, in the case of heights, as far as they could ascertain by judging [*arbitrando*]."[55] These sentences are often taken as inaugurating Renaissance's new interest in measuring. The difference is that Manetti speaks of both taking measurements and estimating while Vasari, even if he wrote with Manetti's biography on his desk, only mentioned the former. The change may indicate that Vasari did not want anyone to question Bramante's measuring. It may also imply that, in Vasari's time, the verb "measuring" had become more inclusive.

In a letter of 1411, four officials from Prato remarked that because they "were not told how to measure," they decided to survey a building as if it corresponded to its plan.[56] Their hesitation reveals a multiplicity of approaches, an openness that does not simply question where to measure, but what to measure. This kind of creativity is often overlooked, even when examining the countless architectural drawings of the Renaissance (more than 3,000 in the Uffizi alone). These drawings can be deceptive in their metric content, as they may have been copied from other surveys or copies of copies (Yerkes 2013: 27–35). This chain of transmission is important in understanding the numerical transmission of measurement. We have already seen how the *Iter* (mis)attributed to Dondi gives the height of St Peter's obelisk as reported by two books and confirmed by a local priest, who is specified as a priest to imply his trustworthiness. Numerical uniformity can be deceptive, as drawings may even mix direct records with secondhand information. In a sheet of the so-called Strozzi codex, the anonymous author notes that most of the measurements were taken by the architect Bernardo della Volpaia whereas those of the cornice were provided by Simone del Pollaiuolo (Zampa 2010: 65).

However, it is not just a matter of architects potentially cutting corners by relying on laborers or other sources. Even when they claim to measure firsthand in order to demonstrate exceptional meticulousness, as de l'Orme did (*Le premier tome*, f. 131 r), there may still be differences in their standards and practices. In my opinion, these differences can be traced back to three main choices architects faced.

The first is whether to measure by touch or sight. An example of touch measuring can be seen in a painting by Andrea Mantegna (Figure 15), where a man is shown pressing a rod against the shaft of a column. This is a straightforward method of establishing a dimensional relationship between

---

[55] Manetti, *Vita*, 67. On Brunelleschi's journey, see Trachtenberg 1985.

[56] Archivio di Stato, Prato: Archivio Datini, n1118, 9300656. Lettera degli Ufficiali del Ceppo di Francesco di Marco Datini, June 5, 1411.

**Figure 15** Andrea Mantegna, *Christ As the Suffering Redeemer*, ca. 1488–1500. Copenhagen, Statens Museum for Kunst. Detail. Photo: author

an object and a standard, such as one column equaling six *braccia*. However, touch measuring was not always the most common choice. When the humanist Angelo Decembrio (1415–67) encountered St. Peter's obelisk, he recorded it as fifty-cubit tall after measuring it "by the eye" (Curran and Grafton 1995: 242). Visual estimates were acceptable even in the marketplace. In Pisa, customers had the option of buying meat "by sight" (*per vistam*) and in Venice, people could purchase wood using this method despite the government's attempts to suppress the practice (Romano 2015: 120). As Manetti stated in his biography of Brunelleschi, visual estimates were not necessarily considered approximate.

This belief led to the measurers' second decision: whether to focus on lengths or angles. Most *libri d'abaco* recommended students concentrate on the latter. For example, an exercise might explain how to determine the height of a distant tower by telling you to stick an arrow into the ground next to you and lower your head so the top of the tower disappears behind the shaft at a point that you then

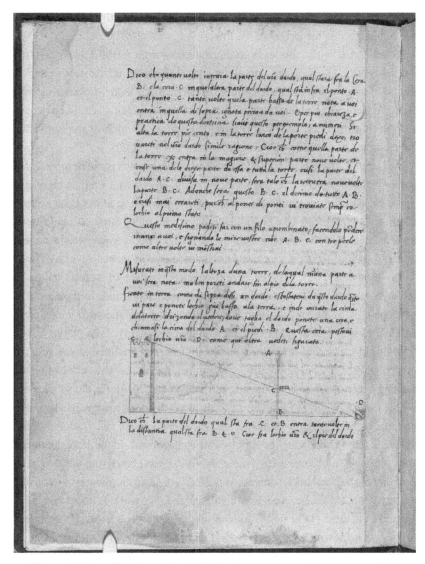

**Figure 16** Leon Battista Alberti, *Ex ludis rerum matehamticarum*, f. 1v. Houghton Library, Harvard University: Ms Typ 422.2. Detail

mark with a piece of wax on the shaft (Figure 16). This method relies on the ancient belief that a line of sight is a geometrical line and that by looking at the top and the base of a tower, you create two laser-like vectors that correspond to the sides of an invisible triangle that converges at your pupil. Since triangles with identical angles are congruent, the segment connecting the ground and the wax mark is proportional to the height of the tower, just as the interval between your eyes and the base of the stick is proportional to the distance between you and the tower. This means that by measuring the three lengths you can access, you can determine the height of the tower.

This exercise, with countless variations, returns from the Middle Ages to the late sixteenth century, when surveyors started applying it also to the underground in order to extract its resources. In his treatise *De Re Metallica* (1556), Georg Agricola argued that "the solid mass of the mountains" could be deconstructed into triangles, which also helped select the location of mining shafts and the gradient of tunnels (Morel 2020).

The belief that the world, both above and below the ground, could be represented by triangles was widely accepted, as the powerful embraced it from an early age. Figure 16 is lifted from a luxurious compilation of measuring games Leon Battista Alberti (1404–72) created for the children of Ferrara's ruling family (Cantile 2005; Wassell 2010: 81). A jurist by training, Alberti viewed geometry as a natural property, stating that "the eye measures quantities with visual rays as if with a pair of dividers."[57] Confident in the geometric nature of vision, surveyors developed various tools to measure angles: the quadrant, the alidade, the astrolabe, the dioptra, or, as they read in Vitruvius, the groma, a staff mounted with a cross with four plumb lines to aid in aligning with distant objects (Lewis 2001).[58]

While not measuring devices per se, plumb lines were essential in ensuring the orthogonality of any operation. Alberti recommends their use when calculating the shooting angle of a cannon (Williams and Bevilacqua 2013). He did so because, like the level, a plumb line is an effective geodetic device: it ties any measuring to the earth, or, better, it grounds measuring. Therefore, I do not take Castiglione and Raphael's self-aggrandizing too seriously when they boast, in the aforementioned letter to Leo X, of inventing a new surveying tool based on the compass. Castiglione and Raphael's compass was simply a geodetic dioptra, a tool that measured the angles between two buildings and the north at the same time. Leonardo da Vinci (1452–1519) used a similar instrument when surveying the fortified perimeter of Cesena around 1502. In one of his drawings (Figure 17), he illustrated the length of each section of the walls and, in fractions, its orientation in relation to the wind rose. For instance, the west wind is identified by the letter *p* for *ponente* (Docci 1987). In 1512, a publication by Gregor Reisch titled *Margarita philosophica* popularized a more sophisticated instrument created by the Freiburg-born cartographer Martin Waldseemüller (1470–1520): the *polimetrum*, which could measure the angles between two objects in space and, simultaneously, the angle of their elevation (Meurer 2007: 1203).

---

[57] Alberti, *On Painting*, 41.
[58] The quadrant and the astrolabe were considered measuring tools already by Dominicus de Clavasio in 1346. See Busard 1965: 522.

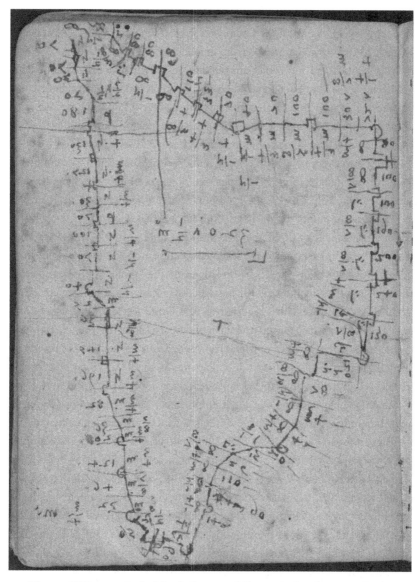

**Figure 17** Leonardo da Vinci, *Survey of Cesena's fortifications*. Paris,
Bibliothèque de l'Institut de France, Manuscrit L, ff. 9v-10r

Following the first treatise on triangulation (Gemma Frisius, *Libellum de
locorum describendum ratione*, 1533), or how to survey an area by measuring
the distance between two points and their angles to a third point, the polimetrum
evolved into what we know as the theodolite. Giovanni Paolo Gallucci (*Della
fabrica*, 1597, ff. 213–14) referred to it as "visorio" in a striking catalog of

measuring instruments that makes no reference to geometrical rules. This separation may reveal less about the fascination these technological objects produced (Bennett 2011: 700) and more about the simplicity of their operations. As Gallucci observes, names and mechanics matter little, as all these tools – Leonardo's, Waldseemüller's, Castiglione and Raphael's, his own – do the same thing: they measure angles and relate them to a stable feature of the earth, whether a wind, the north, the vertical, or simply the soil. Even Frisius's triangulation could be seen as a grounding of Alberti's measuring principles (Hallyn 2008: 104).

Finally, surveyors needed to choose a unit of measurement. To capture the layers of the entablatures of Roman buildings, Antonio da Sangallo and Bernardo della Volpaia took the Florentine *braccio*, which they divided into sixty *minuti* (Frommel 1994: 12).[59] Relying on the standard of one city to measure the structures of another was not uncommon. In 1444, the windows of the cathedral of Orvieto were designed to correspond to two *braccia* from Siena (Milanesi 1854–56: 2, 214). However, the political implications of reading one city's monuments through the standards of another were clear. Cardinal Marcello Cervini suggested to de l'Orme (in Rome between 1533 and 1536) to stop measuring Roman monuments using the French foot and instead employ the local palm, which had been architects' standard of reference since Bramante (Hülsen 1884: 330; Parsons 2016: 91).[60] Even better, the cardinal suggested, would be the ancient Roman foot, as only the foot could restore an ancient building's original proportions. Many Florentines living in Rome continued to use the *braccio* of their hometown because it came close to two Roman feet (Günther 1989: 225–26; Frommel 1994: 57n315). Sometimes architects went even further. When Sebastiano Serlio (1475–1554) published Bramante's tempietto (*Il terzo libro,* 1540: f. 42), he gave its dimensions in ancient Roman feet to invite comparisons with classical monuments, as if the sixteenth-century structure were to be placed among them (Freiberg 2014: 70). This interpretation proved prescient, as Andrea Palladio (1508–80) included Bramante's building in his book on ancient temples (*Quattro Libri*, IV, 64–66).

Alberti was concerned that the creative approaches to standards adopted by architects could make them incomprehensible to outsiders of their circles, including foreigners. He worried that if these standards changed or ceased to exist, it would be difficult for people to understand them without detailed instructions. Alberti recognized the problems raised by ancient metrology in his time would constitute an issue also for future generations. (His worries proved valid, and much of our difficulty when dealing with pre-metric

---

[59]  John Soane Museum, London: Coner Codex, f. 1r, preface.
[60]  De l'Orme, *Le Premier tome*, f. 131r–v.

measurements stems from our lack of knowledge about aspects of their usage.) To address this, in his treatise on architecture, *De Re Aedificatoria*, he articulates all dimensions in abstract proportions, which he calls "modules" (VII.7). When Alberti speaks of the plan of the Tuscan temple (VII.4), for instance, he describes it as five modules by six, with the first three occupied by the porch and each of the remaining ones by a chapel, without mentioning any standard. Alberti consistently relied on the module in his architectural practice, from his first drawing to the last church he built (Borsi 1980: 231; Baldini 1989: 161; Barkan 1999: 30–31).[61] The module also serves as the classificatory guide of the architectural orders, defined by proportions and not stylistic features (Bruschi 2004: 180–81), and even shapes his key architectural values (*numerus, finitio,* and *collocatio*).[62] For Alberti, architecture is mastery of proportional correlations.

While Alberti's practice was indebted to Vitruvius, also a champion of proportional thinking, ratios had been extensively used throughout the Middle Ages (Bork 2016). The tool for constructing modules is the pair of compasses, which records a magnitude without attaching a name to it, thus freeing it from local politics. Together with dividers, compasses came to embody the ethos of measurement in architecture, the production of a dimensional order that remains legible over time. This is why both compasses and dividers appear on the tomb (Figure 18) of the famed architect Andrea Bregno (1418–1506) as a way of celebrating architecture's victory over death (Frommel 2008). They are carved alongside set squares, folding rods, and prisms, showcasing the diversity of measuring practices. Hung on plumb lines, which serve as both literal connectors and metaphorical links for all types of measurement, compasses and dividers are shown in deeper relief at the top and front of a cluster of objects, which seem to acknowledge their subordinate role in fulfilling the cosmological aspirations of proportions.

## 3 Elimination of Matter

### 3.1 Perspective, or Double Measuring

Perspective, or the technique to simulate three-dimensional objects on a picture plane, is a field in which drawing gives way to measuring. Perspectivists do not see an object as having an absolute form; rather, they see its profiles shifting according to their location. A paper square can appear to shrink to a line if its width is all that

---

[61] Alberti's first drawing is Florence: Biblioteca Laurenziana, Ashburnham App. 1828, ff. 56v–57r.

[62] *Numerus* identifies the quantity of elements in a building (*De re aedificatoria* IX.10). *Finitio* has been translated as "proportion" or "dimensional relationship among the parts" (see Paolo Portoghesi's remark in *De re Aedificatoria*, 814n1). *Collocatio* refers to the suitability of an element to its place and optical conditions (IX.7).

**Figure 18** Tomb of Andrea Bregno, 1506. Santa Maria sopra
Minerva, Rome. Photo: author

is visible. Piero della Francesca's treatise (*De prospectiva pingendi*, ca. 1475)
clearly expresses this realization. Painting, Piero states, consists of three parts:
drawing, coloring, and *commensuratio*, a term often translated as "proportion" but
for which Piero provides a more precise definition. *Commensuratio*, Piero
explains, is the method to ensure "the profiles and contours [are] proportionally
sited [*posti*] in their respective places."[63] In other words, *commensuratio* is about
the "siting" of profiles (Bertelli 1991: 52) or, literally, about a measurement within
(*com/cum*) another measurement (*mensuratio*).

Perspective is the product of a double measure. A painter must first ascertain
the distance between an object and its imagined observer, as this distance
determines the perceived size of the object, or its scale. Scale indicates relative
measurement, a dimension that depends on a shifting reference, while size is
thought to indicate objective reference, or a dimension determined by a fixed
standard.[64]

---

[63] Piero della Francesca, *De prospectiva pingendi*, 81.
[64] This is said in the so-called Latin B version of Piero's *De prospectiva pingendi* (19n31).

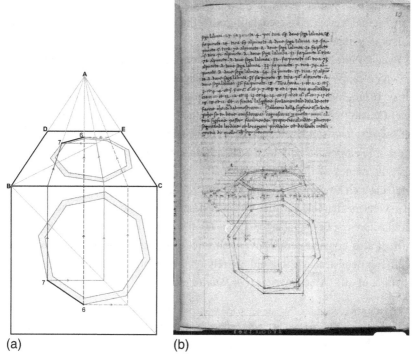

(a)           (b)

**Figure 19** Petrus Pictor Burgensis, *De prospetiva pingendi*, 1472–75, f. 19r. Biblioteca Panizzi, Reggio Emilia: Mss. Regg. A 41/2

Piero's concept of double measuring shapes most of the illustrations of his treatise, which consist of two parts. Take the bottom of the diagram shown in Figure 19, in which Piero outlines an object as to its real dimensions: its size, we could say. Piero places it in a square and traces its diagonal. He translates the object's vertexes horizontally to this diagonal, such as the ones marked 6 and 7, and then transfers these new intersection points vertically until they reach the top side (B–C) of the square. He also translates all vertexes vertically so that on the B–C line each vertex is represented twice, as a vertical coordinate and a horizontal (diagonally reflected) coordinate.

In the second, upper part of the diagram, Piero scales the object in relation to an observer's point of view (marked A). To do this, he constructs a square as if it is receding in space and closed off by side D–E. He traces another diagonal (B–E) and then connects every point on the lower B–C side to point A but stops at the diagonal B–E whenever he is transferring a coordinate reflected by the first diagonal. Finally, he translates this new intersection point horizontally until it reaches the receding line that stems from the other coordinate for the same vertex. This endpoint is the perspectival equivalent of the original vertex. By translating all other vertexes, Piero constructs the object in perspective.

Even if Piero's *De prospectiva pingendi* circulated only in manuscripts, seven of which survive today, Piero's double diagram became a template for many artists (Camerota 2015). On the first page of his *Livre de perspectif*, the painter Jean Cousin (ca. 1490–ca. 1560) labeled the two planes the geometrical plane (*plan geometrial*) and the perspectival plane (*plan perspectif*), which associates the word *perspective* only with the three-dimensional view. "Prospettive" were also the names of the two views of Florence created by Brunelleschi in the 1420s, which he displayed in the very places from which he calculated them, so that viewers marveled at the real world seamlessly continuing the depicted architectures (Trachtenberg 1989: 60–67). Brunelleschi's contemporary Alberti also equated perspective with three-dimensional views, but proposed a different construction that did not rely on the "geometrical" plane.

"First of all," Alberti writes (*On Painting*, 55):

> I draw a rectangle of whatever size I want, which I regard as an open window through which the subject to be painted is seen; and I decide how large I wish the human figures in the painting to be. I divide the height of this man into three parts, which will be proportional to the measure commonly called a *braccio*; for as may be seen from the relationship of his limbs, three *braccia* is just about the average height of a man's body. With this measure, I divide the bottom line of my rectangle into as many parts as it will hold.

Alberti's language is deceptively simple. He states that a man is three *braccia* tall because it was a commonly used phrase in Florence at the time (for instance, see Landino, *Comento*, 1:276). However, he clarifies, Alberti's *braccio* does not refer to the Florentine standard, or to any standard, but to a module calculated based a person's height. Alberti simply uses this familiar term to help the painter adopt the right mindset for depicting the world as it is. In a way, Alberti's *braccio*, which represents an arbitrary module even though the term suggests it is a city's official standard, tries to reconcile the discrepancy between size and scale. By doing this, Alberti argues that even one person's view can be rendered objectively, and I wonder about the widespread effects of this belief – that we can all occupy a single point of view as reality.

The manuals on perspective published in the following two centuries offered new constructions and original applications such as anamorphosis, or the optical illusion whereby a distorted image appears normal when observed from a specific viewpoint (Elkins 1994: 1–44; Massey 2007; Camerota 2016). As knowledge of perspective spread, painters also became aware of its history. In 1583, Giacomo Barozzi da Vignola (in *Le due regole*, 52) called Alberti's single-point perspectival construction "legitimate," a term used to characterize measurement carried out officially, or legally (*misura legittima*), in contrast to a method of his invention. In 1600, the mathematician Guidobaldo del Monte (in *Perspectivae Libri Sex*, 1) argued that perspective served as a means of social and cultural emancipation, since it elevated painting from the mechanical arts, or artisanship, to the liberal arts, or intellectual disciplines (Tiriticco 2013: 193).

Piero had already emphasized the theoretical dimension of perspective. He stressed that its points and lines "are not patent except to the intellect."[65] Many scholars have been intrigued by this abstracting pull and searched for its origins in the reappraisal of Ptolemy's ancient treatise *Geography* (Edgerton 1974; Hankins 1992). In a section dedicated to the principles of cartographic projection, Ptolemy argued that all the world's cities could be represented on a map by coordinates and listed thousands of them. Alberti applied a similar method to Rome when he recorded the coordinates for 176 sites so they could be represented on a map of any scale (Vagnetti 1974). This undertaking has been seen as the inauguration of digitization (Carpo and Furlan 2007), a claim that prompted a reexamination of Ptolemy's fortune and led to the realization that his *Geography* was never rediscovered: it was available to many medieval astrologers and mapmakers who already worked with coordinates (Gautier Dalché 2009: 131). Some revisionists suggest pictorial perspective sparked a renewed interest in Ptolemy's projections and led to the first printed edition of his *Geography* in 1475 (Cattaneo 2011: 72–73).

Indeed, the term *perpectiva* referred to optics since at least the sixth-century Roman philosopher Boethius (Kemp 1978; Kuhn 1990: 120; Elkins 1994: 45). When Manetti attributed the invention of perspective to Brunelleschi, he defined it not as a process of abstraction, but as a representation of the principle "to put down . . . the diminutions and enlargements which appear to the eyes of men from things far away or close at hand" (White 1972: 113). This definition directly links Brunelleschi's views to the measuring exercises by sight discussed in Section 2.

However, medieval *perspectiva* was far from a well-established body of knowledge (Smith 2014: 278–321). Northern European theorists like friars Roger Bacon (1220–92) and Witelo (1230–75) focused on how subjectivity alters visual perception, diverging from Islamic thinkers like Ḥasan Ibn al-Haytham (965–1040), who emphasized light as a geometric body and elaborated on the metaphysics of radiation (Lindberg 1976: 133–46). Florentine masters knew Ibn al-Haytham as Alhacen: sculptor Lorenzo Ghiberti (1378–1455) engaged with translations of his writing (Federici Vescovini 1965).

---

[65] Piero della Francesca, De prospectiva pingendi, 83.

Alhacen's most influential popularizer was Biagio Pelacani (1355–1416), a university professor who taught that the eye could only capture the superficial extensions of bodies in relation to their distance, thereby establishing the key concepts for an understanding of perspective as double measuring (Camerota 2006: 325–26; Belting 2011: 146–50).

Still, perspective is often presented as a view dependent on one point rather than a distance. It has been recognized as a paradigm of fixity: a representation of the world that implies the existence of one subject, or, better, that constructs the subject (Damisch 1994: 23–55). And, as the construction of the subject – with its limits and possibilities – is ultimately a political endeavor, perspective also came to express a political paradigm. More specifically, perspective has been regarded as offering a representation of the world that viewers tacitly accept by inhabiting its (fixed) point of view. In doing so, scholars have taken the technique as expressing the will of the modern state, which forces its citizens into a form of knowledge that preexists them (Trachtenberg 1997: 250–59; Lepenies 2014: 2).

To rediscover perspective as double measuring, rather than a machine of fixity, does not discredit this reading since measurement plays just as powerful a role in erasing the difference between perception and cognition. Any act of measuring, after all, offers an interpretation of the world that claims to pass as the only acceptable one. Alberti recognized such a power in an overlooked section of his treatise on painting. He writes (*On Painting*, 53) that "all things are learned by comparison. There is in comparison a power which enables us to recognize the presence of more or less or just the same." However simple, this statement offers something extraordinary: that comparison is not just a mode of seeing, but a force. Comparisons are not descriptions, but powerful manipulations of the world. When undertaking them, you slip into a form of thinking that foregrounds sameness and makes you forget about differences. As a comparison between magnitudes (one man's height = three *braccia*), measuring presses you into searching for the similarities between breathing humans and abstract modules.

One of the ways in which measuring accomplished this transformation is by desensitizing people to materiality. Florence may have been particularly suited to perspectival thinking not only because of its emphasis on mathematical education, but also because it expanded the application of its main standard, the *braccio da panno*, beyond the cloth trade in which it originated. In Brunelleschi's time, Florentines grew up in a world where measuring was already a homogenizing practice: fabrics, people's height, and the built environment were all quantified one way. By proposing to take the *braccio* as a pictorial module, Alberti continued a practice that must have been second nature to him.

The indifference of measuring to materiality cannot be generalized. While most Tuscan cities adopted Florence's system – the citizens of Volterra, for instance, also measured buildings with lengths for cloth (Caciagli 1978) – Milan never saw one standard as prevailing over the others. In other cities throughout Europe, quantification was subjected to material appraisal. It is important to stress this alternative to remind us that there is nothing necessary in the Florentine trajectory, despite the paradigmatic role it has acquired today.

After all, like measurement, perspective is not something that captures the world as it is (Damisch 2002: 120). Serlio's book about perspective (his second) captures the abstract space of tiled interiors, staircases, and stone door frames. Similarly, in a perspectival landscape (Figure 20), Cousin privileges sharp corners and barrel vaults. The faraway city is a still life of prisms – a dome, an obelisk, a column that looks severed rather than broken. Leaves and trees are visual trinkets: fleeting accidents, dabs of ink. The Venetian architect Daniele Barbaro (1514–70) even states that the perspectival rendering of vegetation requires much consideration for "trees, mountains, landscapes … are things that, because of their nature, are indeterminate."[66] Foliage is rendered through flashes of lights and out-of-focus recesses, effects measuring cannot capture.

## 3.2 Body Molds

It must have been difficult for an artist working in Italy around the middle of the fifteenth century to not think of the human body in terms of measurements. All the manuals that have survived from that time encourage them to study the body dimensionally. For example, a handbook written by the fourteenth-century painter Cennino Cennini (*Libro*: 38–39),[67] suggests drawing a face as if made of three equal parts – the forehead, the chin, and the nose – which Cennini confusingly also calls the "face." In his notes on art, which he left unfinished when he died in 1455, Ghiberti (*Commentarii*, 300–05) provides a list of proportions between a man's height and other parts of his body, like the face (or the distance from the chin to the hairline), which he takes as being equal to one-tenth of a man's height. A hand (from the wrist to the tip of the middle finger) has the same ratio, while the foot corresponds to one-sixth.

Renaissance artists developed various proportional systems. Vasari mentions how Parri Spinelli (1387–1453) painted bodies that were 50 percent taller than those of his predecessors.[68] Instead of focusing on the convergence toward one

---

[66] Barbaro, *La Pratica*, 158.
[67] Cennini's manual is known through two manuscripts, both in Florence. One (Biblioteca Medicea Laurenziana, Florence: Plut. 78.23) was copied in 1437, the other (Riccardiana library, Florence: Ms. 2190) in the early seventeenth century.
[68] Vasari, *Vite*, 290. Vasari says Spinelli's heights were twelve "heads" versus an average of eight.

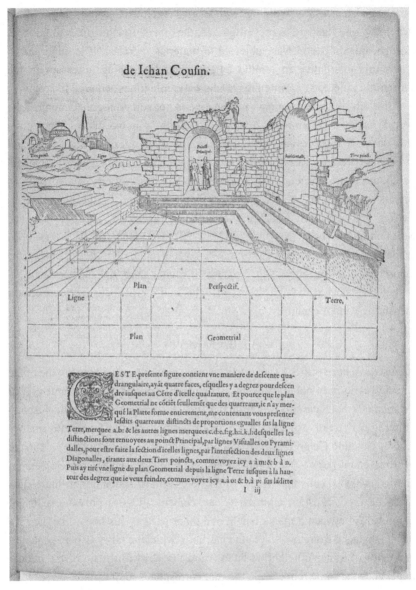

de Iehan Coufin.

**Figure 20** Jean Cousin, *Livre de Perspective*, 1560, f. 81

prevalent canon (as suggested in Panofsky 1940), it is important to note the lack of uniformity among these systems. However, for the sole purpose of orientation, I recommend memorizing a ratio of eight heads for a man's height (with one "head" equal to the distance from the chin to the top of the head). While arbitrary, this choice provides a reference point that can be useful when exploring the diverse landscape of modular canons.

The 1:8 proportion, however, returns frequently. Landino's comment on Dante's *Comedy* (*Comento*: 1, 276) refers to it when speaking of a man's height. Jean Cousin the Younger, son of the homonym perspectivist, employed it when teaching portraiture (*Livre de pourtraicture*, 1608, f. 34 v–35 r). The ratio even served as a standard for teaching how to design capital letters.[69]

Drawing from Vitruvius (3.3.10, 4.1.8), early modern architects constructed a theory of orders where the Ionic column corresponded to eight times its base, while the Tuscan corresponded to six, the Doric seven, the Corinthian nine, and the Composite ten (Günther 1989: 157). Serlio canonized this system by illustrating it in the opening of his first publication in 1537 (Figure 21), creating a sort of "architectural grammar" (Summerson 1980: 10–27) that many European theorists modified but never invalidated (Onians 1988; Carpo 2001: 42–56; Bruschi 2004: 176–235). Barbaro, for instance, spoke in favor of using "head" rather than "diameter" in architecture, stating that "it is within reason that the measures of things, as well as their reasons, have been taken from human parts, and it is reasonable that the measure of everything is derived from the head since the value of all human feelings is placed in the head."[70]

The goal of these proportional norms, historians insist (Panofsky 1955: 95–96), was to achieve beauty. However, to put the matter in these terms flirts with tautology since many Renaissance authors define beauty as harmony between parts. Alberti recommends that painters strive for *concinnitas*, a dimensional consonance that participates in the mathematical order of the cosmos (Tavernon 1998: 43–44). As Plato explains in *Timaeus* (35b-5-35c2), a text around which Alberti shaped much of his thinking (Hendrix 2011), the demiurge gave form to the universe in proportion. For this reason, it is somewhat misleading to speak of proportions as merely producing aesthetic pleasure: for Platonists, proportions were means to participate in the demiurge's creation. Ghiberti, like Palladio (Payne 1999: 170–87), spoke of necessity: retrieving and respecting human proportions is a natural imperative.[71] If we follow this reasoning, measurement ceases to be a quantifying technique and becomes a search for righteousness.

Classical sources played an important role in legitimizing the idea of measurement as a quest. Pliny (34.65) emphasized that the great sculptor Lysippos altered the canon first proposed by Polykleitos in his lost treatise Κανών (or "standard," on which Leftwich 1995) and created figures that seemed taller,

---

[69] Cresci, *Essemplare*, unnumbered: "imperò chi le fa condurre alla proportione et misura di otto teste."

[70] Barbaro, *I Dieci libri*, 63.     [71] Ghiberti, *Commentarii*, 299, 300, and 304.

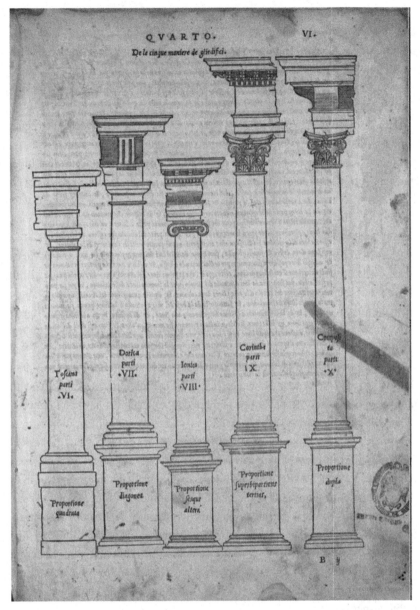

**Figure 21** Sebastiano Serlio, *Regole generali di architettura sopra le cinque maniere de gli edifici* [also known as *Quarto Libro*] (Venice, Marcolini 1537), f. 6r

taking into account the observer's perception (Barkan 1999: 253–57). According to the painter-turned-author Giovanni Paolo Lomazzo (*Trattato*, 29–30), Michelangelo also learned the importance of perception when he measured the Dioscuri in Rome and found that their heads were much larger than their bodies, a proportion he repeated in his statue of David. And by stating how a man could be inscribed by both a circle and a square, Vitruvius (3.1.2) set human proportions as the result of a tension between incompatible geometrical shapes.

Many fifteenth-century architects (Mariano Taccola, Francesco di Giorgio, Fra Giocondo) tried to illustrate the Vitruvian pronouncement (Sgarbi 1993), with historians identifying the most elegant solution in Leonardo's so-called Vitruvian Man (Ungers 1994: 309). Leonardo not only separates the centers of the square and the circle but also relates them to the penis and the navel, the end of the umbilical cord, thus providing a reproductive rationale for a study of man's body at its peak, ready to continue the chain of procreation (Figure 22).

However, despite its graphic accomplishment, Leonardo's study is not definitive. His figure is suspended between not only two geometrical shapes but also two proportional systems. Leonardo first listed below the drawing the dimensions that he himself recorded in male bodies and then transcribed above it Vitruvius's proportions (Lugli 2019b). It is as if Leonardo used this drawing to work out whether the two could converge – whether the proportions in Vitruvius (3.1.7–8 and 4.1) could be found in nature. As they could not, Leonardo took the foot to be one seventh of a man's height, thus overlooking Vitruvius's definition as one sixth – he eventually abandoned the project of systematizing human dimensions in a treatise, of which the Vitruvian Man could have served as an illustration (Marani 2009).

In part due to the attention Leonardo's twofold approach has attracted over the past century, historians have tended to classify artists as taking measurements from either nature or literary sources. They have distinguished when Ghiberti (*Commentarii*, 309) follows Vitruvius and when he does not, implying that departures from Vitruvius are motivated by a preference for real-life observations (Ciocci 2016: 125). Some have pointed to a drawing by Antonio da Sangallo the Younger (1484–1546) in which most of the space is dedicated to illustrating a canon of his own invention (Zöllner 1995). In this drawing (Figure 23), Antonio shrinks the Vitruvian diagrams to the side as if to indicate their unimportance. He also presents the human foot as made of 14 *dita* rather than Vitruvius's 16 and a man's height as 120 *dita* (as he writes behind the man's head) rather than the traditional 96 (that is, eight heads). However, analyses based on the culture/nature dichotomy are ultimately self-defeating because they overlook the pressure under which culture and nature are laminated. This is demonstrated by the fact that Antonio does not measure the actual body in its curves, but rather projects the extremes of the limbs onto an imaginary line that cuts through the sacrum, the bone at the base of the spine, and is demarcated by

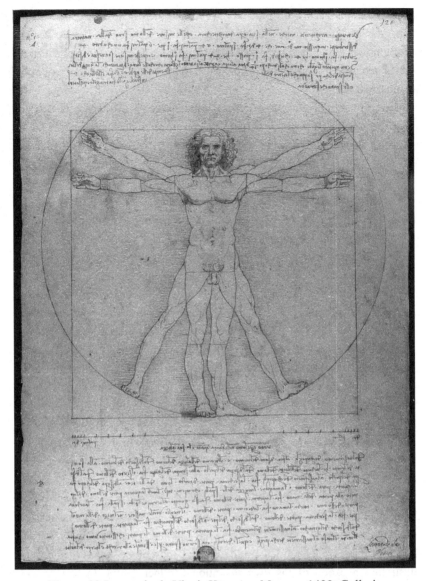

**Figure 22** Leonardo da Vinci, *Vitruvian Man*, ca. 1490. Gallerie dell'Accademia, Venice

segments. Furthermore, even though Antonio downplays Vitruvian proportions, he approaches the human body through a fascination with numerical perfection. Couldn't a man's height be 119 *dita* rather than 120?

What are *dita* anyway? What did the units employed in these canons – *palmi*, *piedi*, and *braccia* – mean to people in the fifteenth and sixteenth centuries? It is

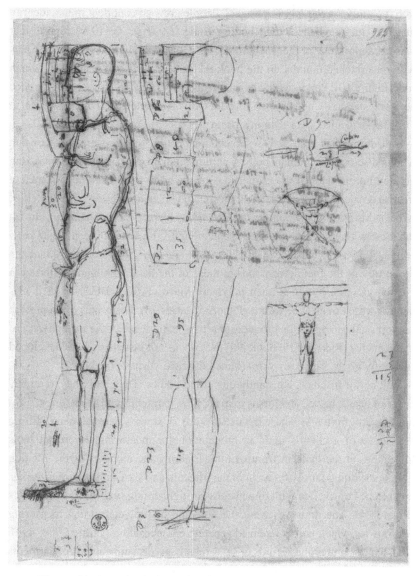

**Figure 23** Antonio da Sangallo il Giovane, *The Measures of Man*,
ca. 1528. Gabinetto dei Disegni e delle Stampe, Gallerie degli Uffizi,
Florence: n. A 1249r

often unclear. They may refer to human limbs, ancient standards, or even
modules. Vitruvius did not think there was any difference between them. He
states (3.1.5) measurement standards were taken from the human body and were
one with it. Humanists like Fonzio (*Letters*, 148–54) endorsed this ambivalence.
Seventh-century church authority Isidore of Seville (*Etymologiarum* 15.15.1–2)

said it plainly: "a *digitum* is a finger." People grew so confident in this identity that they measured with their bodies. Budé (*De Asse*, f. 119 v) reports that masons approximated the standard of one foot by drawing together their fists with outstretched thumbs. In the book that first advertised the ancient Roman foot (Figure 10), Porzio warned against this practice by stressing the difference between standards and limbs: "the foot of my homeland, which we use to measure space, is longer than my 16 fingers."[72]

Still, humanists read across subjects, expecting to discover a system that would disclose the human body's participation in measurement's totalizing project. Porzio fetched the proportions of the body from Columella's ancient treatise on agriculture. The ancient physician Galen, an admirer of Polykleitos, wrote in his *De usu partium* (*On the Usefulness of the Parts of the Body*), among the most widely taught works on medicine until the sixteenth century (*Opera omnia*, 4:354–55; Kusukawa 2012: 184, 204), that "it is necessary that the proportion of the foot corresponds to those of the hand." Philander referred to a canon devised by the Roman polymath Varro (116–26 BCE), even if it is unclear which treatise he meant (Panofsky 1955: 76). Historians often present proportional canons as the products of artists' experience of the metaphysics of mathematics (Rykwert 1996: 68–95). Yet it was not just artists who developed such lofty goals. The body was scanned metrically across the board.

Tailors, for instance, constantly quantified bodies. They took the circumferences of heads, necks, and torsos to make hats, garments, and accessories.[73] An illumination from a Milanese treatise (Figure 7) shows a garment maker lifting the sleeve of a client's tunic in preparation for measuring, his metal tools glistening on the table in front of him. Entering the archives of the Medici, Florence's ruling family for most of the fifteenth and sixteenth centuries, brings up sketches of liveries with dimensions for tight-fitting breeches and doublets (Figure 24). The drawings were the outcome of time-consuming measuring sessions for which tailors received separate compensation (Currie 2009: 496). And, while statutes and records of sales mostly give us dimensions of garments and bodies (Tosi Brandi 2017: 99), tailors were also encouraged to think about their work proportionally.

In 1464, the astronomer Johannes Müller (1436–76), also known as Regiomontanus, gave a lecture in which he encouraged artisans to use proportions in their work.[74] Thirty years later, Pacioli (*Summa*, f. 68 v; *Divina proportione*, f. 16 r) disagreed with him, stating tailors were already doing so, but, like the best artisans, should strive to relate even the smallest details, such as stitches, to the

---

[72] Porzio, *De sestertio*, f. 32r.    [73] See, for instance, Porro Lambertenghi 1878, 5: 638–39, 665.
[74] Regiomontanus, *Oratio*, lines 326–27.

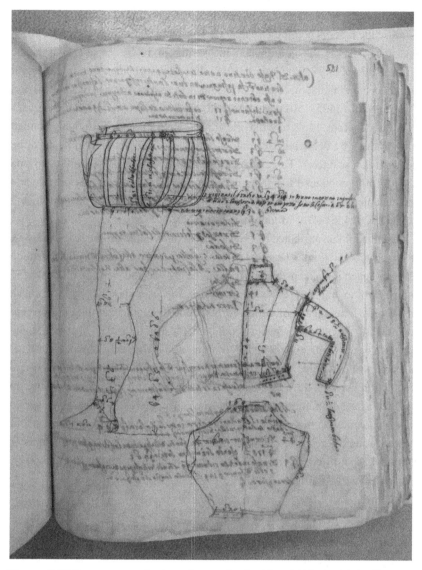

**Figure 24** Measurements for breeches and a doublet, 1593. Archivio di Stato, Florence: Guardaroba medicea 143, f. 521r. Photo: author

sizes of their clothes. Pacioli's suggestion of approaching every gesture proportionally was not a new idea, as it was already circulating among elite groups. He was simply bringing this mindset to the attention of everyday makers.

An earlier example of this attitude comes from the master fencer Filippo Dardi, a teacher at the University of Bologna. In 1434, before Alberti completed his treatise on painting, he instructed his students to think of their bodies proportionally. In a letter, he states that "geometry conforms to the art of fencing because the latter is nothing else than measuring itself."[75] Like dancing, which was theorized as the coordinated measuring of bodies, space, and music (Baxandall 1972: 77–78; Castelli 1987), Dardi saw geometry as foundational for understanding the mechanics of the body in space. Another fencing master, Filippo Vadi (1425–1501), also opened his *De Arte Gladiatora Dimicandi*, composed before 1487 (around the time Leonardo started studying human proportions), by declaring "fencing is born out of geometry" and ought to be considered a science.[76] Three generations later, the Milanese Camillo Agrippa (1520–1600) continued this thought by writing (*Trattato* 1.2) that the fencer's movements are "governed only by points, lines, tempos, and measurement" (Lincoln 2014, 61–114; Mondschein 2014).

One illustration, attributed to Leonardo's admirer Carlo Urbino (ca. 1525–85), deconstructs the lunge (Figure 25). It shows how far a fencer's outstretched arm can reach if he keeps his left foot on the ground and steps farther with the other. Urbino highlights the range of the fencer's shoulder with a curve marked by letters, each of which corresponds to another on the horizon line to indicate how far the fencer would hit (Marinelli 1981). But while the diagram advertises the benefits of thinking about the body dimensionally, it also blurs the difference between limbs and swords. Measuring makes no distinction between flesh and metal: it produces a reality in which physicality is given as a continuum of points and lines. The approach unleashed a series of seventeenth-century treatises that formalized measured movements in space (Jaquet, Verelst, and Dawson 2015), most notably by the Dutch master Gérard Thibault (ca. 1574–1627) and the Spanish fencer Luys Pacheco de Narváez (1570–1640).

### 3.3 *Misura* As Morals

Urbino's illustrations for Agrippa's treatise are strikingly uniform in size, age, musculature, and equipment. They are less representations of actual fighters than their sublimations into ideas of warriors. Such regularity was perhaps inspired by Vegetius, the late fourth-century author of a much-read treatise on military institutions (Settia 2008: 39), who reports Roman recruits ought to be six feet tall (*De Re militari* 1.5). Only in one instance does Agrippa concede that fencers' bodies could vary. At the end of the first book, he discusses the affliction of being short, whose only resource is patience. If you happen to be

---

[75] Archivio di Stato, Bologna, Comune, Governo, busta 318, "Riformagioni e provvigioni," Serie miscellanea, busta 5. Translation by Trevor Dean.

[76] Rome, Biblioteca Nazionale Centrale, Ms. Vitt. Em. 1324, f. 4r.

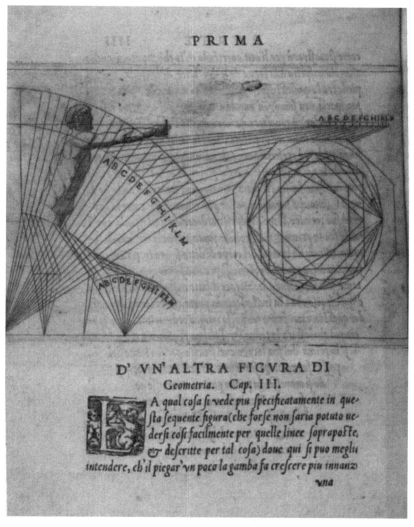

**Figure 25** Carlo Urbino, The measurements of the lunge. In Camillo Agrippa, *Trattato di Scientia d'arme*, 1553, f. 4v

small, wait for your opponent to expose his body and then burst into a lunge (Agrippa, *Trattato*, f. 38 v). Which is a way to confirm Agrippa's tenet – the lunge is always the answer – while stressing the need for identical bodies to actualize his vision of fencing as a geometrical activity. Agrippa does not standardize bodies so much as he implies them, as did many of the artists who dealt with human proportions.

When Leonardo took the measurements that eventually led to the Vitruvian Man (figure 22), he did not analyze the limbs of hundreds of men, but two. He even tells us their names – Trezzo and Caravaggio – and that he chose them because they had "greater grace" (Nepi Sciré 1992: 220). He was even more selective when studying the proportions of horses for he focused on only one specimen, Siciliano, the favorite destrier of his patron, Galeazzo Sanseverino (Panfosky 1940: 42). Leonardo's findings were then tweaked from the start: he selected paragon bodies, thus depriving his reflections of any general validity.

Leon Battista Alberti did something similar when listing human proportions in his treatise on sculpture. Alberti claims he derived the measurements from "many bodies, considered to be the most beautiful by those who know, and took from each and all their dimensions, which I then compared one with another and, leaving out of account the extremes on both sides, I took the mean figures [*mediocritas*]."[77] Yet his claim of direct experience has been questioned given that his measurements correspond to the canons employed by Florentine artisans at the time (Aiken 1980: 81). Alberti may have simply written down what he saw artists doing. (Notice also his reliance on "those who know" – that is, authorities, who, like for standards, determine what is right.) Interestingly, he credits his method to Zeuxis, the Greek painter who, when tasked with a portrait of Helen of Troy, combined features from beautiful women. By referring to this tale, reported by Cicero (*De inventione* 2.1) and mentioned by Pliny (35.36), Alberti reinforces the impression that a perfect body could be produced through selection.

Alberti's vocabulary is particularly expressive. By speaking of *mediocritas*, he entered moral grounds for the term was indissociable from Thomas Aquinas' definition as a mark of virtue.[78] Horace (*De Carmina* 2.10) and Cicero (*De Officiis* 1.36) amplified this characterization when spurring their readers to aspire for the mean since *mediocritas* was precious and worthy of love. In his etiquette manual *The Courtier*, Castiglione (1478–1529) broadcasted *mediocritas* as the principle that guarantees safety in every aspect of life.[79] It is in also in this cautionary sense that swordsman Angelo Viggiani dal Montone (d. 1552) celebrated *mediocritas* as a key quality of the fencer, who must measure his steps when facing an opponent (*Lo schermo*, f. 7 r).

*Mediocritas* and measure were often conflated. But while passing for a mathematical concept, *mediocritas* was not always obtained mathematically. Its meaning of rejection of extremes prevailed over its capacity to identify the middle point. However, while the concept of *mediocritas* was as subjective as beauty (and Alberti considered the two equivalent), its mathematical dimension turned *mediocritas* into a link between geometry and morality. To understand

---

[77] Alberti, *On Painting and on Sculpture*, 135.

[78] Thomas Aquinas, *Commentarii in Decem Libro ethicorum Aristotelis*, book 2, lectio 7.

[79] Castiglione, *Il Cortegiano* 2.41.

the widespread appeal of measuring in the early modern world, it is important to recuperate the moral dimension that geometry always expressed.

"Measure [*misura*] is a virtue that makes all our ornaments and all our doing without defect," wrote Brunetto Latini (1220–94) in a medieval encyclopedia that was still in print in the sixteenth century.[80] Aquinas thought proportioning was an ethical process, since a deed is virtuous when it unfolds through words and actions that are commensurate with it (Eco 2022: 37–68). Vasari (*Vite* 4:9) criticizes artists for not exercising judgment (*giudizio*) when sizing their figures, thus showing that he took dimensions as expressive of control. Piero took the word *commensuratio* from Aristotle, who used it to speak of the temperature equilibrium that maintains health in bodies.[81] When applied to physiology, this reasoning implies, measure is a principle of good life.

This moral dimension was especially clear to artist Albrecht Dürer (1471–1528) who, at the beginning of his treatise on human proportions (*Underweysung der messung*, 1525), defines measurement as both "proportion" and "self-measure" (Filippi 2008). Prior to this, Dürer and his collaborators worked on a ten-foot-tall engraving of a triumphal arch to honor the achievements of Holy Roman Emperor Maximilian I (Silver 1994: 60). The only scroll included in the engraving bears the message "Halt mass," a call for moderation that Maximilian had inscribed on many of his possessions (Terjanian 2019: 196). Believing that abstract virtue and practical accomplishments are interconnected, Dürer may have chosen to gild the scroll, the only element in the print to receive such treatment, to celebrate Maximilian's recent (1510) decree to standardize the imperial gold coinage using the weight of the Venetian ducat, Europe's most esteemed currency (Stahl 2012: 48). The move reminded local rulers that the emperor held the sole authority to set standards and was significant because it came during a time of economic fluctuation due to the discovery of silver mines (Grierson 1975: 30–31; Cipolla 1989: 19–20; Giráldéz 2019: 19–21).

So important was *mediocritas* to qualify moral conduct that Lomazzo (1538–92), an admirer of Dürer's measurement studies, thought that those who got baptized should be depicted with softer proportions. It's not that after their conversion "long limbs become short, or fat ones thin," he explains (*Idea*, 143), but the moral salvation that came with baptism also expresses itself proportionally as if a certain angular discrepancy softened.

Lomazzo's statement appears less eccentric when considering that Christ was often thought of as embodying the perfect human form. A rich theological tradition presented him as having an ultimate body with proper stature,

---

[80] Latini, *Il Tesoro*, f. 153v.  [81] Aristotle, *Topics* 6.2, 1496, f. 233v.

straight posture, and perfectly "proportionate limbs."[82] However, while theologians hardly elaborated on Christ's dimensions, tiptoeing around Christ's vague biblical description as "the most handsome of the sons of mankind" (Psalms 45:2), devotions for the height of Christ (*mensura Christi*) supplied precise measurements, thus promising a tangible relationship with God's son.

During the late fifteenth century, manuscripts, crosses, and prayer rolls across Europe reproduced segments believed to correspond to one-twelfth or one-fifteenth of Christ's height (Lugli 2019a: 145–52). Look at the line every day or wear the ribbon around your body, reads a caption to one of these segments in New York's Morgan Library, and you would be healed or spared violent death (Skemer 2006: 228–30; Murray Jones and Olsan 2015: 426).[83] Ribbons cut to the length of Christ's feet, side wound, and the bodies of other miracle-working saints were thought to pass their healing properties through quantification.

These beliefs persisted throughout the Renaissance, and it wasn't until the final session of the Council of Trent in 1563 that bishops were given the authority to prohibit what some considered superstition (as stated by the bishop of Valencia, in Christian 1981: 246n33). It was acceptable to produce devotional measurements as long as they helped to remember the saints, rather than flaunt protection from harm. The Shroud is an emblematic case of this. As a mechanical impression of Christ's outlines on a veil, it developed a cult on the belief that size does not change over time (Casper 2021: 102–03). Church authorities encouraged reproductions of its dimensions, as seen in commemorative engravings (Figure 26) produced since its first public display in 1578, which included bold-faced letters indicating the extremes of segments to reconstruct the true dimensions of the cloth and Christ's body. (As expected, it was proportionate: Christ's height corresponded to four times the width of his shoulders.)

Bishops had a financial incentive in promoting contact relics, such as reproductions of Christ's height and the Virgin Mary's shoe sole, as they came with indulgences. This fueled a thriving market of imitators, which was not disbanded until 1678 by Pope Innocent XI (Bianchi Giovini 1865: 2:571–74). The difficulty of eradicating these practices was not only due to their popularity, but to also the belief, more insidious and perhaps even more prevalent, that quantifying a body held some virtue.

These considerations are crucial in understanding a final point. It was not that in the Renaissance, people who were considered perfect were measured and their proportions served as a reference, as Alberti suggests. The opposite seems to have been the case: some bodies were considered perfect if they displayed

---

[82] Alfonso De Villegas, *Nuovo leggendario*, 493. On earlier commentaries on Christ's appearance, see Bacci 2014: 86–87.

[83] New York, Pierpont Morgan Library, n. 16529.

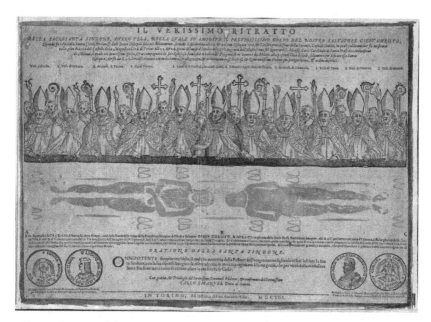

**Figure 26** Broadsheet reproducing the Turin shroud showing the imprint of Christ, 1608. Printed by Giovanni Antonio Silva. London, British Museum, 1913, 0528.120. Photo: London, British Museum Images

perfect ratios. It is the detection of these ratios that gave some men "greater grace," as Leonardo wrote when discussing the models he measured for his Vitruvian Man (Figure 22).[84] Barbaro is one of the few writers who recognized this relationship, noting that ancient writers paid attention to grace when discussing proportional systems, which could also be found in the "perfect bodies" of athletic twenty-year-olds.[85] On the other hand, Marsilio Ficino (*Theologia platonica*, 2:138) expresses ambivalence when he says: "measure is the beauty of all things beautiful." This statement illustrates the circularity of beauty, which is uncertain whether it is detected or projected, but, without a doubt, can only be accessed through measurement.

The abstraction of bodies through measurement was the first step in accessing the ideal world of beauty. Writers encouraged readers to record their heights with a rod, the precise location of moles, and the geometrical shapes formed by the creases on their palms (Porter 2005). In a miscellanea that also gained

---

[84] Grace is God's gift: both an emanation of beauty and a steer directing Christians toward virtue, on which Mac Carthy 2020: 37.

[85] See also Barbaro, *I Dieci libri*, 63: "Besides proportion, the ancients searched for grace . . . I am speaking of perfect bodies because other measurements are found in a puerile body, a slim body, a fat body, or a weak body."

popularity in Italy (Bognolo 2012: 261), the Spanish writer Pedro Mexía (1497–1551) suggested checking whether your face had Vitruvian proportions. Use your thumb as a standard, he wrote (*Silva*, 157), and see if it matches the size of your lips and your nose. (There is some flexibility here as you could subtract the nail). Mexía conceded that Vitruvian proportions were not likely to be found in every face, but declared that "whoever gets closer to this rule will be the most handsome." The Italian poet Lodovico Castelvetro (1505–71) followed suit when stating (*Poetica*, 161) that a man is beautiful if he "comes close to the perfect measure of men," warning that anyone "could be considered a monster if he exceeded the usual measure [*misura usitata*] of the human species." The harmful social and psychological repercussions of this delusion continue to affect us today.

## 4 Elimination of Interpretation

### 4.1 Universal Men

"Weights, measures, and money are, of course, the foundations of commerce upon which rests the entire structure of trade," wrote the Spanish Jesuit Juan de Mariana (*A Treatise*, 31) in 1609. Such confidence came from Aristotle's *Ethics*, which merchants could read starting in 1550 thanks to Bernardo Segni's first Italian translation (Garin 1986: 215; Bianchi 2009). And according to Aristotle, money was "the measure of anything:" the standard that enabled the comparison of different goods, from "shoes to houses to food" (Segni, *L'Ethica*, 241).

Measurement and money were the equalizers of the world, and it is in this light that I read the pages on currencies, weights, and length standards that fill the mercantile manuals of the fifteenth and sixteenth centuries. Those lists were less conversion tables than declarations that any object could be exchanged with others, and even between merchants who did not speak the same language. Known as *tariffe*, these inventories cataloged the goods sold at each harbor and provided information about payment times and trading customs (Borlandi 1963: 90–97). They explained whether almonds were sold with or without shells, whether cinnamon was available in Paris (it was), and whether it was more convenient to change money in London rather than in Bruges (the latter seems to have been the case).

These examples come from Giorgio di Lorenzo Chiarini's *Libro di mercatantie et usanze de paesi (Book concerning the Trade and Customs of Various Places)*, which compares the standards of European harbors with those of Italy's major hubs: Florence, Venice, and Genoa. It states, for instance, that 1 London ell corresponds to 1 1/2 Venetian braccia, while 6 Venetian *braccia da tela* make 25 ells of Bruges. The text was written around 1458 and circulated in manuscript form, before being printed in 1481, and again in 1497 and 1498. Pacioli included it, word for word, in his famous work, the *Summa*. Throughout the sixteenth century, its fame was only challenged by Bartolomeo di Paxi's *Tariffa dei pesi* (1503), which was reprinted in 1511, 1521, and 1557. Thanks to a much-improved layout, this text made it easier to retrieve information on a greater number of harbors, even though it mostly related their standards to Venice, presenting it as the sole center of a dense network.

Comparing Chiarini's and di Paxi's books reveals that neither was comprehensive or systematic. Chiarini links Florence to Bruges; di Paxi does not. Each manual constructed different maps of trade and thus oriented merchants' interests, shaping opinions about what was possible and where. The creativity of these manuals is particularly clear when considering abridgments like Girolamo Tagliente's much-reprinted *Libro d'abaco*, which heavily compresses information about Venice's weights and currency (Riccardi 1870, 2:482–89), and foreign manuals such as Lorenz Meder's *Handelbuch* (1558), which omits information about the north of Europe to create a network between German and Italian centers (Harreld 2010: 18).

Measurement conversions defined trading networks. Their fundamental role is demonstrated by a map of twenty-seven seaports probably created by the Majorcan Arnaldo Domenech for Siena (Figure 27). The cities' locations are approximate (Venice is shown as being closer to Tunis than Sicily) as merchants were not deterred by distances: it was their job to pursue lucrative deals by overcoming practical difficulties and exploiting cultural imbalances (Spufford 2003: 342–48). What the map does is illustrate a desire of connectivity, with each city's conversion between its own weights and those of another harbor represented in a circular vignette (Ristow and Skelton 1977: 3–4). The lines connecting the ports stem from these conversion equations, demonstrating measurement conversions, rather than geography, guided trading patterns.

The sixteenth century saw an explosion in the publication of *tariffe*. New charts or new editions of old charts came out almost every month, not only to correct misprints but also to provide information about fluctuating currencies and political changes (Hoock and Jeannin 1991, 1:402–22). The Ottomans, who took over Constantinople in 1453, slowly replaced Byzantine weights and measures with those of central Asia (Inalcik 1983). The *Tresoir van de maten* of 1590 addressed the Antwerp merchants who took refuge in Amsterdam during the Dutch revolts (De rusysscher 2018: 153–54).

Italian manuals, usually printed in Venice, were particularly requested since Italian served as a sort of lingua franca of the Mediterranean. Chanceries drew contracts in that language even when no Italian was involved (Cremona 1997).

**Figure 27** Arnald Domenech, Map of seaports, 1484. Library of Congress, Washington, DC: G5672.M4P5 1484 .D6. Photo: Library of Congress, Geography and Map Division

The poet Girolamo Muzio (1496–1576) proudly confirmed (*Battaglia*, f. 192 v) that "you will find our language everywhere." A trader from Oderzo, near Treviso, even tried to get rid of his dialectal inflections to facilitate business (Brown 2020: 16).

Together with *tariffe*, these linguistic efforts made the Mediterranean Sea appear as a shrinking pond. Maps contributed to this perception by speeding the identification of harbors and the calculation of navigation routes (Carlton 2015: 75–99). If in the Middle Ages, large-scale trade was possible for only a few powerful family businesses and cities (Hunt 1994: 76–100, Goldthwaite 2008: 38–48), early modern tools instilled a new enthusiasm, encapsulated by *Della mercatura e del mercante perfetto* (*On Trade and On the Perfect Merchant*), penned by the Croatian Benedikt Kotruljević (1416–69).

Kotruljević argues for the rise of a new type of trader: a "most universal man [*huomo universalissimo*] gifted with every faculty, capable of understanding and dealing with every type [*generatione*] of men."[86] The modern merchant lives free from local customs and aligns himself to a new, worldly horizon (Piotrowicz 2013) for which measurement conversions provide an essential framework.

In half a century, these ideas spread so widely that the Venetian politician Girolamo Priuli (1486–1567) complained his fellow citizens' obsession with landownership had turned the younger generations into provincial "country-men, without any experience of the things of the world."[87] A merchant, he claimed, ought to embrace scale by entering foreign partnerships and investing in numerous centers – Florence, Rome, Avignon – proud of having "a finger in many places" (Lopez 1955: 414; Tucci 1973). Some scholars have remarked that such scale-defying advice came from merchants who did not travel (Kedar 1976: 24–41; Tangheroni 1996: 293). The epithet "universal merchant" is a euphemism for a sedentary manager exploiting the labor of others.

The story of Kotruljević's treatise loosely corresponds to the chronological arc of this Element. Although it was written in 1458, it was not published until 1572, allowing its ideas to reach a wider audience (Tucci 1990–91). The law student-turned-canon-turned-writer Tommaso Garzoni (1549–89) built upon these ideas when he stated (in *La Piazza*, 1:660) that "trading should be considered a vulgar thing if on a small scale; if, however, it is on a grand scale, importing many things from different parts of the world and distributing them without fraud to all, then it should not be despised." Even if Garzoni was quoting Cicero (*De Officiis* 1.42) in this statement, the citation took on a different meaning in the Catholic states where he lived. The church officially approved of trading if merchants contributed to the distribution of wealth (Muzzarelli 2019). Moralists such as Garzoni insisted that, as long as merchants increased people's well-being, they could counteract the greed inherent in their profession (Tucci 1973: 347–48).

Kotruljević was openly devout. "Neither king nor prince ... has as much faith ... as the merchant" (*Della mercatura*, f. 66 r–v). Like God-fearing

---

[86] Kotruljević/Cotrugli, *Della mercatura*, ff. 68r–v.    [87] Priuli. *I diarii*, 50.

Orlando, whose statue was erected in Dubrovnik (Figure 6) around the time he was born there, a merchant must exhibit his piousness for only divine law provides the "respect for the equality of justice when buying and selling" (*Della mercatura,* f. 59 r–v). Here we have it: an admission that sees no conflict between trading and religion. Only by embracing a transcendental scope does the universal merchant come to believe in the very possibility of justice.

Historians have identified a number of models of masculinity that aspired to a sort of virtuous universality once reserved for knights and saints (Burckhardt 1890: 136–38; Penrose 1952: 67). Jurisconsults, experts of the *ius commune* that served as legal basis across Europe, felt at ease internationally (Kelly 1988: 89). In 1564, the controversial alchemist Leonardo Fioravanti (*Dello specchio di scientia universale,* f. 95 v–96 r) celebrated the *merciaro* (a figure in between apothecary and drysalter) as more knowledgeable than lawyers since he ought to know "thousands upon thousands of goods … from many countries in the world" whereas jurists only needed to know some laws. Palladio insisted architecture speaks a "universal" language (Wittkower 1944: 107), and the rapidity by which his precepts spread through Europe proved him right (Harris 1994: 1–17). Like Alberti, Palladio reported the proportions of orders by using a module that corresponded to the diameter of the base of the column rather than "specific standards, that is, standards specific to a city" (*Quattro libri,* I, 16). His choice subtly exposes the intrinsic flaw to standards: while they lay claim to absolute sameness – measurement "bring universal justice and quiet" according to fellow architect Ligorio – their variety and perishability preclude the achievement of those aspirations.[88]

Some worked to grant measurement standards the universal validity of the module. Palladio's teacher, the diplomat Gian Giorgio Trissino (1478–1550), tried to convince Pope Paul III (1469–1549) to "correct and reorder the currencies, the weights, and the measurement of the whole of Italy."[89] He thought such a patent demonstration of progress would not only add to the pontiff's glory but also provoke a crisis among the Lutherans and Ottomans. How could foreign nations continue pursuing separatist agendas from a ruler who made the world whole again? A few decades later, the economist Gasparo Scaruffi (1519–84) proposed the creation of a universal mint, and thus a unified weighing system, that would issue one currency, "as if the world were one city or monarchy."[90] The idea betrays knowledge of Greek historian Polybius (264–146 BCE), who celebrated the cities of Morea for having adopted the same weights, measures, and laws so that the Peloponnese

---

[88] Ligorio, *Libro dei pesi*, 3.    [89] Cited in Morsolin 1894: 426–27.
[90] Scaruffi, *L'Altinonfo*, f. 55v.

peninsula "lacked nothing to appear like a city but one circle of walls around all its citizens."[91]

These universal proposals were directed at rulers and their counselors. In *Della ragione di Stato* (82), the political thinker Giovanni Botero (1544–1617) stated only the prince had the authority to issue laws, as well as fighting frauds, "minting coins, institute measures, and weights, and tariffs." A secretary of the prominent Borromeo family, Botero studied with de Mariana and claimed (*A Treatise*, 12) that "the first thing that brought kings to eminence was their protection of citizens from the impending enemy storms when their people were mustered around their standards." It is for this reason that the French jurist Jean Bodin (1530–96) traced (*Six Books* 1.10) the origin of France's civilizing process in the medieval kings who "resolved that there would be only one system of weights and measures." (He is referring to Philip the Fair, Philip the Tall, and Louis XI.) The association of measurement and enlightening rulership was merely confirmed by the many reports of European travelers to the Americas, who, as the Portuguese bishop Jerónimo Osório summarized (*De Rebus Emmanuelis*, f. 53 v), (mistakenly) claimed the natives of Brazil "have neither weights nor measures, and are not subject of any king."

Fueled by the idea that unifying measurements increased civilization, in 1565, the Crown of Poland elected the Kraków ell as its official standard (Kula 1986: 117). Following Hernán Cortés's ordinances of 1524, the viceroys of New Spain issued decrees to force all conquered cities to adopt the Spanish weights and measures (Carrera Stampa 1949: 3–6). In Section 1, we saw how France undertook similar initiatives. Yet none of them brought immediate change. Countrymen resisted the new standards, which could not just be imposed, for measurements are not tools but modes of seeing and thus require a process of reeducation to take hold in society.

In 1572, the Habsburg government discovered a tremendous disparity between the grain measures in the Low Countries, leading to the realization of the ineffectiveness of its regulations (Dijkman 2011: 212–14). It is also because of this revelation that Stevin wrote *De Thiende* (1585), the pamphlet in which he proposed to divide standards decimally. Without a simple, unified system, merchants resigned themselves to learning all the laws, customs, and weights along their routes, as if they could "see what the sailors and pilgrims of all time saw" (Muzio, *Il gentilhuomo*, 281). Throughout the sixteenth century, lofty aspirations of universality paralleled a pragmatic acceptance of the world's diversity. Standards aspiring to the

---

[91] *Polibio*, f. 91r–v.

international legibility of the module – that is, standards that resisted both local customs and subjective interpretations – materialized only when Mouton (1670) and, a few years later, Dutch scientist Christiaan Huygens (*Horologium Oscillatorium*, 17 and 106) put forward proposals for measurements extracted from natural laws and thus, they believed, applicable to any place on earth (Yoder 1988: 154).

## 4.2 Life-Size

This "countering of subjectivity" (Daston and Galison 2007: 36) was driven by a belief that attributed measuring to nature. Whether nature was thought as shaped by God (who "disposed of all things by measure, number, and weight") or as an independent force (that "gives form to matter from within," as Ficino said), measurement was viewed as a feature of the world rather than a personal interpretation of it (Hadot 2006: 24).

Ghiberti (*I commentari*, 82) praised ancient sculptors for thoroughly studying nature and thus "making art with the measure that nature offers." Alberti (*On Painting*, 33) noted that artists' reliance on ratios in painting "shows how this noble and beautiful art arises from roots within nature herself." It doesn't matter whether the reasoning is circular – whether art is praised for reproducing natural dimensions or for revealing that it operates like nature through proportional ordering. As the humanist Benedetto Varchi (1503–65) reasoned (*Lezzioni*, 9 v–10 r), neither nature nor dimensions like width, length, and depth can ever be demonstrated; people can only accept their existence.

Ghiberti's and Alberti's remarks have been read as invitations to directly rediscover nature's proportions, rather than relying on the pattern books that artists revered. Their advice paved the way for a new concept, the life-size, which, however, was not formalized until a century later when Vasari praised any depicted figure that was "as large as the living thing" (*grande quanto il vivo*).[92]

Art critics popularized Vasari's expression,[93] as did scientific academies by commissioning botanical illustrations, anatomical plates, and any image that stood in for the real thing (Kusukawa 2012: 107; Fend 2019). The painter Joshua Reynolds (1723–92) recognized that "figures the size of life" were a quintessential achievement of Italian art and advised his students to work at the same scale, including as many details as possible, even though the English

---

[92] Vasari, *Vite*, vol. 1, p. 475; vol. 2, pp. 114, 293, 406, 459; vol. 6, pp. 80, 92, 476, 483.

[93] Francesco Sansovino, *Venetia città nobilissima et singolare* (1581), 133; Raffaello Borghini, *Il riposo* (1584), 512, 584, and 609.

preferred smaller pictures (Northcote 1819: 1, 46–47 and 138–39). Alberti (*On Painting*, 101) had already acknowledged that depictions "as near as possible in size to the actual object you wish to represent" served as paragons for painters wanting to test their representational flawlessness.

Endorsed by Reynolds, the first president of London's Royal Academy, "life-size" has become a trope among English-speaking art historians to talk about all Italian Renaissance art. However, it is worth noting that when Ghiberti and Alberti spoke of "misura al naturale," they were referring to the generic dimensions found in nature. Vasari, on the other hand, introduced the concept of "life-size" to accommodate aspirations of aliveness. Vivid lifelikeness was not an uncommon goal among medieval artists (Pinkus 2014), but Vasari saw it as a new characteristic of the works of painters such as Michelangelo (1465–1564) and Titian (ca. 1489–1576), who not only created a perspectival space in a continuum with their viewers but also aimed to engage them emotionally (Puttfarken 2000, 123–47). In the same way Thomas Aquinas (*Summa* 2.1, q.35) believed emotions resided in the human soul (King 2009), viewers in the sixteenth century often felt a strong affection when they believed they were encountering the souls of others. Intellectuals like Muzio (*Avvertimenti morali*, 177–78) even encouraged men to embrace their emotions and express them through crying. How else could anyone show to have accepted the fleetingness of mortal life?

During the Renaissance, death was the invisible horizon toward which the concept of the life-size unfolds. This was a departure from earlier instances, such as in Ottonian art, which promoted crucifixes "extended like a human figure" in response to debates about the role of imagery in the liturgy (Fricke 2015: 105n379). Historians have traced the origins of the Italian life-size back to medieval votive gifts, such as candles that were the same height as a person, hand casts, or amounts of grain that corresponded to the weight of a baby (Bacci 2000: 175–82; Maniura 2009). These gifts were believed to have the power to extend the lives of the petitioners in death through measurement. This faith in measurement's ability to connect the tangible world to divine forces was widely held, as demonstrated by the *mensura Christi* and other contact relics. As such, it should be considered a primary driving force behind the contemporary creation of life-size art (Didi-Huberman 1998), possibly more so than a desire for naturalism, which is often cited as the main motivation of the Renaissance.

The life-size as an artistic value developed out of the sculptures of actual bodies artists created to address their patrons' concerns about salvation (Panzanelli 2008: 18; Kren 2018: 25). According to Cennini (*Libro*, 205), artists were expected to master casting techniques, and scholars like Olariu (2009: 88–90) have observed how casting affected the style in sculpture from the thirteenth century. By the 1400s, casting was no longer solely used for devotional purposes but impacted painting.

We know artists Francesco Squarcione (1397–1468) in Padua and Neri di Bicci (1419–91) in Florence collected casts as teaching aids (Ames-Lewis 2000: 52–58, Marchand 2010). In 1428, when Ghiberti was lent a classical gem, he did not hesitate to cast it and circulate its replicas (Dacos 1989: 72–73). The renowned physician Andreas Vesalius (1514–64) used gesso molds to teach anatomy in 1540 (Heseler 1959: 139), and it is possible that Vesalius's popular lectures, during which he also dissected corpses, contributed to Vasari's appreciation of the useful immediacy of the life-size.

Casts, which only reproduced the form of the original objects, could provide a similar aesthetic experience for those who valued form over matter, and thus attained a significance almost equal to their sources. Vasari recounts (*Vite*, 6:145) how sculptor Baccio Bandinelli (1493–1560) was commissioned a full-size copy of the famous Laocoon for the king of France. After numerous studies, a 1:1 cartoon, and a wax model, Bandinelli produced such a high-quality replica that in 1524 it was sent to Florence rather than France (Barkan 1999: 276–79). The king waited twenty more years to receive casts of Roman statuary thanks to Raphael's pupil Francesco Primaticcio (1503–70) who then made bronzes out of them, the first collection of its kind (Haskell and Penny 1981: 2–6; Bensoussan 2019).

In 1587, art critic Giovanni Battista Armenini (*De veri precetti*, 63) praised the lightweight nature of plaster casts, stating they could be "brought to any country." Like measurement standards, casts conveyed exact dimensions across space. "What is more amazing," marveled Alberti (*On Sculpture*, 125), "is that you could hew out and make half the statue on the Paros Island and the other half in Lunigiana [near the Carrara marble quarry] in such a way that the joints and connecting points of all the parts will fit together to make the complete figure and correspond to the models used."

Alberti wrote these words to introduce three new tools for measuring bodies: the *exempeda*, the *normae mobiles*, and the *finitorium* (Figure 28). The exempeda is a ruler as long as a person and is divided into 600 *minuti* to detect even the smallest differences. The normae are two sliding set squares that gauge the widths of arms, legs, and torsos. Finally, the finitorium is a movable radius with an adjustable sliding plumb line. When placed on top of a sculpture, the finitorium can determine the three-dimensional location of any point on the sculpture's surface by adjusting the position of the plumb line. These three tools work together to create a kind of encasement that surveys the body like a laser scanner. It should be clear by now that, for Alberti, measuring is a form of intangible casting.

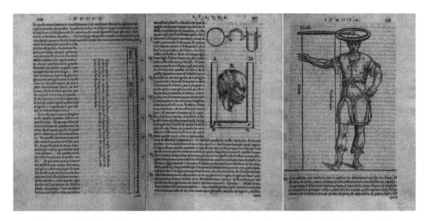

**Figure 28** The Florentine braccio, the normae, and the finitorium. In
L. B. Alberti, *Opuscoli morali*, ed. and tr. C. Bartoli (Venice: Franceschi, 1568),
pp. 294, 297, and 299.

Alberti explicitly connects the two practices. In *On Sculpture* (123), he
imagines covering a statue by Phidias "with clay or wax so that it became
a thick column" and then piercing through it at a set height and depth to retrieve
an eye pupil. Rather than wrapping tape measures around a body like a tailor
(Figures 7 and 24), Alberti sought points on the surface of a body by piercing the
column of airspace around it. Similarly, the Neapolitan humanist Pomponio
Gaurico (1482–1530) suggested (in *De scultura*: 106–07) projecting a body's
outline onto a base. Their methods were similar because both Alberti and
Gaurico followed the methods of mathematicians in measuring the surface of
an irregular, impenetrable object, such as a forest. Frame its area with
a rectangle, wrote Tartaglia (*General Trattato*, f. 29 v–30 r), and take measurements from it to the perimeter (Figure 29). This is also what architects did when
measuring cornices with a plumb line (as shown in the top right corner of
Figure 8a), hanging at the outermost edge as a temporary reference (Bortolozzi
2020, cat. 81).

But to derive architects and sculptors' practices from surveyors' is
a simplification for all their methods found an origin in measurement
standards, many of which were displayed on walls like incisions
(Figures 4 and 5), as if the products of casting. Measuring rods and brick
molds were validated by matching them to carvings, similar to how casts
relate to their molds. Their conceptual connection was recorded by the
grammarian Francesco Alunno (*La Fabrica*, 197 v–198 r), for whom
*improntare* (to cast) was semantically one with *stampare* (to print), *sigillo*

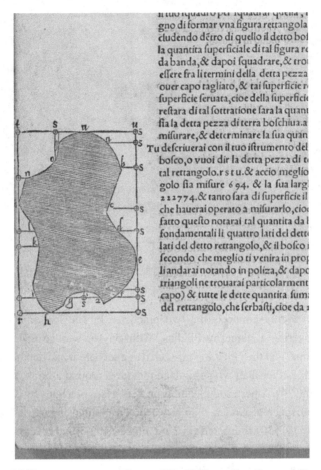

**Figure 29** How to measure a forest. Nicolò Tartaglia, *General Trattato di numeri, et misure*, 1566, f. 29v

(seal), *regula* (ruler) and even *riga* (line) and *lineamenti* (human features), a chain of concepts that expands our understanding of the connotations of measurement in the Renaissance.

## 4.3 Precision and Complexity: A Conclusion

The belief that casting produced a perfect replica of the original, however, was called into question by the engraver Enea Vico (1523–67). Vico stressed (*Discorsi*, 66) that casting left the copy with a certain material residue that needed to be scraped away manually. Alberti's belief that measuring erased distance was also disputed. In 1464, when the duke of Burgundy asked

Francesco Sforza (1401–66) for three armors, the Milanese ruler did not request his ally's measurements. Instead, he sent the trusted armorer Francesco Missaglia. It was a diplomatic gesture, but also a practical necessity. Missaglia had to measure the duke to produce tight-fitting armor (Martens 1952: 226–27). Secondhand dimensions were not precise enough.

The etymology of the word *precision* (Latin: *praecisio*) refers to cutting (*caedere*). Classical authors like Cicero (*Ad Herennium* 4.30) considered it an abrupt, even if deliberate, stop in an oration (Bione 1910: 45). Dante (*Paradise* 17.34–35, 30.30) mentions precision only in relation to speech or singing, and humanists continued this usage even as the word took on another meaning, out of metaphysics. Thomas Aquinas defined *praecisio* as the measure of God's perfection, from which humans are cut off (LeNotre 2016: 136–37). He did so when commenting on Aristotle (*De Caelo* 1.6), who postulated that there could be no proportion between the infinite and the finite. The axiom moved Nicholas of Cusa to conclude that any human operation, no matter how carefully executed, could not capture God's design (Cassirer 1963: 23). Precision could only be defined in the negative, as falling short from absolute truth (Ragno 2011: 121).

Today, precision retains something of this ontological crisis as it designates the variance between human attempts to represent truth. It is often mistaken for "accuracy," a term which was first recorded in 1644 (McIntosh 2020: 101) and identifies one effort's proximity to truth, regardless of other attempts (Teller 2013: 192). Accuracy is then to precision what size is to scale. As size assumes the stability of the reference standard while scale considers it relative, accuracy indicates proximity to a fixed value while precision captures the differences between its interpretations.

As mentioned, artists increased their accuracy by devising new tools. Alberti created the exempeda of 600 units. Antonio da Sangallo and Bernardo della Volpaia split a *braccio* into 60 *minuti* rather than the customary 20 *soldi*. (They may have thought that going further – that is, dividing a *soldo* into *denari* – would produce units unnecessarily small to describe stone carvings). Scholarship claims architects were even more precise at the drawing board. Giuliano da Sangallo sketched the Coliseum "a punto" (Günther 1988: 230; Frommel 1994: 8), as did Michelangelo's collaborators (Mussolin 2007: 216). But at this point, again, the vocabulary is confusing because "a punto" both denoted the twentieth part of a *denaro* and, because of that, connoted a job "accurately" done.[94] As I do not see how these drawings are sensible to a variance of 0.02 mm, the length of the punto standard, I take the specification as simply meaning carefulness. After all, there is no other evidence that

---

[94] *Dizionario della Crusca*, 1612, 69.

Renaissance architects employed tools with that level of precision. Among the first to rely on the punto was Galileo Galilei in 1602 (Drake 1986: 302). But even Galileo used it rarely, and a contemporary math textbook (Lorenzo Forestani's *Pratica d'arithmetica e geometria*, 1603), does not even mention it.

Still, some mathematicians strove for a new sense of minuteness. Girolamo Cattaneo (doc. 1540–84) proposed (*Opera del misurare*: 2, 10 v) to split the *braccio* of his hometown, Brescia, into 1,728 *momenti* (Frangioni 1992: 87). His division was impractical but, as his compatriot Tartaglia explained (*General trattato*, part 2, f. 158 r), practicality was not the focus Cattaneo wanted to break down standards to a point no one could physically measure. Previous sections showed how architects recast dimensions around universally legible modules; now we see the parallel effort to make measurements intangible, like numbers.

Tartaglia was not the first to acknowledge a tension between geometry and arithmetic. Was a line a series of points in a row or, as Alberti wondered (*Elementi*, 50), the stretching of a point? Garzoni (*La piazza universale*, 1585, 1:253) thought these queries represented the only disagreements between measurers, an enviably harmonious group to his eyes, for geometry was the search of agreement.

Garzoni gave this definition in an encyclopedia of human activities in which "geometers, measurers, surveyors, and weighers" pursue solutions to the same issues, regardless of their fields of application. Measurers assisted the sciences, the arts, trade, and even religious exegesis, moving across them as mercenaries fought on different battles. His categorization is useful for rediscovering some early modern biographies in a new light. Consider Francesco del Borgo (1415–68). He is often called an architect after completing the fifteenth-century Palazzo Venezia (Frommel 1998). Yet, Francesco da Borgo built little in his life. Instead, he took on many roles (customs officer, papal accountant, church surveyor) whose common denominator is found in measuring only.

Francesco del Borgo's identification as an architect is strengthened by historicist tendencies for measurements eventually fell under architects' purview. The trajectory of Milan's guild of engineers and land surveyors (*Universitas ingenierorum et agrimensorum Mediolani*), Europe's first, is emblematic of this takeover (Liva 2008: 10). The association was founded on proficiency in measuring. The title may spell engineers and surveyors out, but the statutes explain that, in line with Garzoni's observation, the association was for anyone who measured "both on a paper and on the field," as well as those who estimated properties (Zanetti 2017: 336). In 1533, Cesare Cesariano, painter, translator of Vitruvius, and surveyor, became a member (Repishti 2007). Yet, from 1558, the surveyors' spot was taken by architects, who, together with engineers, claimed to be the professionals with the necessary mathematical knowledge to operate measuring tools (Verin 1993; Fiocca 1998).

Even mathematicians loosened their grip over measuring when arithmetic dethroned geometry as their leading preoccupation (Høyrup 1994). While the great mathematician Rafael Bombelli (1526–72) insisted (L' *Algebra*, 1579: 648) arithmetic and geometry are complementary, as "each serves as a demonstration to the other," the English philosopher Thomas Hobbes (1588–1679) called geometry a pointless pursuit (Jesseph 1993; Beeley and Scriba 2012: 234–35). Isaac Newton (1643–1727) accepted measurements only when perfectly accurate, which is a way to say: as long as he could ignore their practice and consider its outcomes as flawless as numbers (Dunlop 2012: 99–100). The definitive pull came from Joseph-Louis Lagrange (1736–1813), who in *Méchanique analitique* (1788) made no use of diagrams: all his demonstrations relied on formulas (Galletto and Barberis 2006). As Lagrange explains, geometrical constructions require verbose commentaries (I reproduced three in this Element when discussing Alberti's, Piero della Francesca's, and Agrippa's diagrams), and words hinder mathematics' universalist aims. Only by disposing of geometry could mathematicians overcome linguistic barriers and open their field to progress. English mathematician John Wallis (1616–1703) voiced a minority opinion in *Mathesis Universalis* (1657), when stating that numbers too express a relationship, like magnitudes, and thus fall short of their alleged self-sufficiency (Michell 1993: 188–89).

This waning interest in geometry also characterized Galileo Galilei's life (1564–1642). At twenty-three, he gave a passionate lecture at the Accademia Fiorentina on the measurements of Dante's inferno (*Due lezioni*, 1588). Despite a warning from the poet Annibale Caro that "poetry does not go with the measurement of calipers" (*Apologia*, 55), celebrations of Dante's mathematical consistence were common at the time (Biagioli 1993: 117–18). Galileo, for instance, calculated that the giants Dante encountered in hell were forty-four *braccia* tall, whereas Dante's height was only three. In doing so, he confirmed Manetti's previous reconstruction of hell and Alberti's belief (in *On Painting*, 51) that an average man's height was three braccia, boosting local pride. Galileo also confirmed Alberti's belief that proportions do not change with size: the tall and muscular Hercules was simply an enlarged version of the common man Evander.

By the time he was forty-seven, however, Galileo changed his mind. Were a giant fourteen times the size of an average person, their bones would not be able to support their weight and would break. "Who wanted to keep the proportions between the limbs of an ordinary man in an enormous Giant should . . . find a much harder and more resistant matter to make his bones."[95]

---

[95] Galileo, *Discorsi*, 129. While published in 1638, the *Discorsi* were written around 1611.

That is, in order for giants to have proportions like those of a regular person, they would need to have skeletons of denser materials, like iron, or have thicker bone shafts to support their increased size (Figure 30). This would make them appear much, much stouter.

Galileo's reasonings took a stab at Palladio, who thought that bridges, like columns, could be scaled up or down irrespective of their material (Di Pasquale 2001: 19–88). Differently from architects who took measuring as an aid to form, Galileo believed in using measuring as a way to understand the properties of matter. Between 1597 and 1599, he developed a graduated compass that enabled soldiers to calculate the angle and distance at which a cannon should be fired,

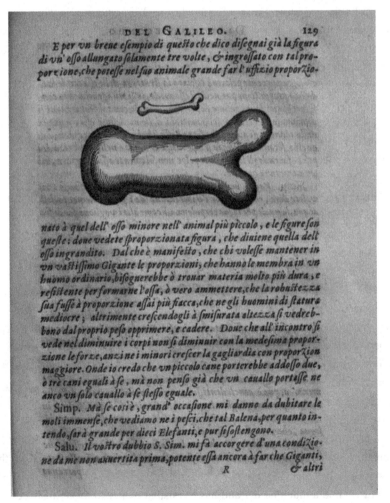

**Figure 30** The bone of an average man and the bone of a giant. Galileo Galilei, *Discorsi e dimostrazioni matematiche*, 1638, p. 129

taking into consideration the size and material of the cannonballs (Camerota 2004: 30). Metric accuracy was not just a quest for precision but also to ensure that observations made from different perspectives and at different scales could be all held in balance like the wheels of a machine (the metaphor is from Descartes, on which Laudan 1981: 27–58). The great metallurgist Vannoccio Biringuccio (1480–1539) had previously recognized this goal when emphasizing the importance of both weighing and measuring the size of a bell at each phase of its manufacturing process to ensure the quality of the final product (*Pirotechnia*, ff. 207 v–208 r).

The assignment of importance to matter reduced the influence of interpretation and emphasized the crucial role of time. The three elimination processes I highlighted as characteristic of Renaissance measuring – the belief that measuring could ignore the passage of time, be applied to any material, and transcend personal interpretation – went through a reconfiguration as measurers began to verify their observations by comparing them to other results. While measuring still involved estimating the relationship between two quantities, this process of cross-examination helped limit any measurement errors to the values established by other measurements. It did not completely eradicate interpretation, or what scientists call "error," but it did reduce its scalar order.

The recognition of such entanglement, which marked the beginning of a new epistemology, led to the development of the laboratory as a space for carefully controlled experimentation. In the laboratory, nature was not just being described in its general values but as to the inner workings of its particulars (Smith 2006; Morris 2015). The laboratory was a place in which nature was recreated under strict control protocols from which the external world was shunned and where everything was custom-made (Baird 2004: 68). The great German metallurgist Lazarus Ercker (1528?–93) even provided instructions (in *Beschreibung*, ff. 36 r–39 r) for constructing, testing, and preserving scales, rather than sending them to Nuremberg, allowing readers to bypass guild and civic regulations.

If Alberti, Leonardo, and other fifteenth-century makers who preoccupied themselves with measurement thought of ways to counter the variability of standards without openly challenging governments, this was no longer the case in the seventeenth century. Retreating to their laboratories, metallurgists, alchemists, and, later, chemists began to develop their own measurement systems and precision standards in private, sharing them with each other rather than with the public. For example, in 1664, the Royal Society in London requested the Rhenish standard from Huygens rather than the city of Cologne (Yoder 1988: 154). Similarly, as we saw, in the following century, Charles Marie de la Condamine, a member of the Académie des sciences in Paris, provided a toise to Ximenes rather than the Florentine government. In these cases, city administrations were on the receiving end of such exchanges, but did not initiate them, as was the case with Stevin, the Flemish engineer who proposed to base measurement on the decimal system.

Governments benefited from scientists' findings, as did craft guilds, factories, and the other actors of proto-industrialism, who embraced technological innovation to meet the demands of an increasingly international market (Pfister 2008). Yet, by the late sixteenth century, the ethos of measurements changed significantly. Rather than being a shared pursuit of equity, measurements became tools designed specifically for the needs of a small, privileged group (Heilbron 1990; Porter 1995; Barker 2022). Such an elite made them available to governments and the rest of the population only after making sure that their views of the world would not be questioned.

# Bibliography

Primary Sources (*Editiones Principes*, Early Modern Reprints, and Critical Editions)

Agrippa, C. *Trattato di scientia d'arme*. Rome: Antonio Blado, 1553.

Alberti, L. B. *Elementi di pittura*. In G. Mancini, ed., *Opera inedita*. Florence, 1890, pp. 48–65.

Alberti, L. B. *De re aedificatoria*, ed. G. Orlandi and P. Portoghesi. Milan: Il Polifilo, 1966.

Alberti, L. B. *On Painting and On Sculpture*, tr. C. Grayson. London: Phaidon, 1972.

Alunno, F. *La Fabrica del Mondo*. Venice: Niccolò de Bascarini, 1548.

Aristotle. *L'Ethica d'Aristotele tradotta in volgar Fiorentino da Bernardo Segni*. Florence: Lorenzo Torrentino, 1550.

Armenini, G. B. *De veri precetti della pittura*. Ravenna: Francesco Tabaldini, 1587.

Bernardino da Siena. *Prediche volgari sul campo di Siena 1427*, ed. C. Delcorno, 2 vols. Milan: Rusconi, 1989.

Barbaro, D. *I Dieci libri dell'architecturra di M. Vitruvio*. Venice: Marcolini, 1556.

Barbaro, D. *La pratica della perspettiva*. Venice: Camillo & Rutilio Borgominieri, 1568.

Barozzi da Vignola, G. *Le due regole della prospettiva practica*. Rome: Zanetti, 1583.

Bartolo da Sassoferrato, La tiberiade. Ed. Claudio Tobalduzi. Rome: Gigliotto, 1587.

Biondo, F. *De Roma Instaurata*. Brescia: 1503.

Biringuccio, V. *Pirotechnia*. Venice: Geronimo Giglio, 1559.

Bombelli, R. *L'Algebra*. Bologna: Giovanni Rossi, 1579.

Borghini, V. *Discorsi*, 2 vols. Florence: Giunti, 1584–85.

Botero, G. *Della ragion di Stato*. Venice: Gioliti, 1589.

Bracciolini, P. *De Varietate Fortunae*. In R. Valentini and G. Zucchetti, eds., *Codice topografico della Città di Roma*. Vol. 4. Rome: Istituto Italiano Storico per il Medio Evo, 1953, pp. 230–45.

Budé, G. *De Asse et Partibus Eius (L'as et ses fractions. Livres I–III)*, ed. L. A. Sanchi. Geneva: Droz, 2018.

Caracciolo, R. *Spechio de la fede*. Venice, 1495.

Caro, A. *Apologia degli accademici di Banchi di Roma contro Lodovico Castelvetro*. Florence, 1819.

Castelvetro, L. *Poetica d'Aristotele*. Basel: Pietro de Sedabonis, 1576.

Castiglione, B. *Il Cortegiano*. Venice: Aldo Romano e Andrea d'Asola, 1528.

Cattaneo, G. *Opera del misurare*. Brescia, 1572.

Cennino Cennini. *Libro dell'arte*, ed. M. Serchi. Florence: Le Monnier, 1999.

Chacon, P. *Toletani Opuscula*. Rome: Typographia Vaticana, 1608.

Chiarini, G. di Lorenzo. *Libro che tracta di mercantie et usanze di altri paesi*. Florence: Francesco di Dino di Jacopo, 1481.

Cicero. *Ad C. Herennium de ratione dicendi*, ed. H. Caplan. Cambridge, MA: Harvard University Press, 1954.

Connan, F. *Commentarii juris civilis Libri X*. Paris: Vascosanus, 1553.

*The Correspondence of Erasmus*, tr. C. Fantazzi and ed. J. M. Estes, vol. 18 (Letters 2472 to 2634, April 1531–March 1532). Toronto: University of Toronto Press, 2018.

Cresci, G. F. *Essemplare di più sorti lettere*. Rome, 1560.

Cyriac of Ancona. *Later Travels*, ed. and tr. E. W. Bodnar. Cambridge, MA: Harvard University Press, 2004.

De' Bianchi, T. *Cronaca Modenese*, ed. C. Borghi. Parma: Fiaccadori, 1865.

De la Condamine, C. M. Extrait d'un Journal de Voyage an Italie. *Histoire de l'Académie Royale des Sciences avec les mémoires de mathématique et de physique* 1755 (1762): 336–411.

Del Monte, G. *Perspectivae Libri Sex*. Pesaro: Hieronymus Concordia, 1600.

De l'Orme, P. *Le Premier tome de l'Architecture*. Paris: Federic Morel, 1567.

De Marchi, F. *Architettura Militare*, ed. L. Marini. Rome: M. de Romanis, 1810.

De Mariana, J. *A Treatise on the Alteration of Money (1609)*, tr. P. T. Brannan. Grand Rapids, MI: Christian's Library Press, 2011.

De Villegas, A. *Nuovo leggendario della vita, e fatti di N.S. Giesu Christo*. Venice: Guerra, 1593.

Dondi, G. *Iter Romanum*. In R. Valentini and G. Zucchetti, eds., *Codice topografico della Città di Roma*. Vol. 4. Rome: Istituto Italiano Storico per il Medio Evo, 1953, pp. 65–73.

Duprat, P. *Lexicon Ivris Civilis Et Canonici*. Paris, 1576.

Ercker, L. *Beschreibung allerfurnemisten mineralischen Ertzt unnd Bergwercks Arten*. Frankfurt: Schmidt for Feyrabendt, 1580.

Erizzo, S. *I dialoghi di Platone*. Venice: Giovanni Varisco and Company, 1574.

Ficino, M. *Teologia Platonica*, ed. M. Schiavone. Bologna: Zanichelli, 1965.

Fioravanti, L. *Dello specchio di scientia universale*. Venice: Valgrisi, 1564.

Fonzio, B. *Letters to Friends*, ed. A. Daneloni and tr. M. Davies. Cambridge, MA: Harvard University Press, 2011.

Fournier, P. S. *Manuel typographique*. Paris: par l'Auteur, 1764.

Frontinus. *De Aquaeductu Urbis Romae*, ed. R. H. Rodgers. Cambridge: Cambridge University Press, 2004.

Galen, C. De usu partium. In K. G. Kühn, ed., *Opera omnia*. Vol. 4. Leipzig: Karl Knobloch, 1821–33, pp.346–66.

Galilei, G. *Discorsi e dimostrazioni matematiche*. Leiden: Elzevier, 1638.

Galilei, G. *Due lezioni all'Accademia fiorentina circa la figura, sito e grandezza dell'inferno di Dante*. In *Opere di Galileo Galilei*, Vol. 9, ed. A. Favaro. Florence: Giunti, 1899, pp.29–57.

Gallucci, G. P. *Della fabrica et vso di diuersi stromenti di astronomia, et cosmografia*. Venice: Roberto Meietti, 1597.

Garzoni, T. *La Piazza universale di tutte le professioni del mondo*, ed. G. B. Bronzini. Florence: L. S. Olschki, 1996.

Gauricus, P. *De Sculptura* (1504), ed. A. Chastel and R. Klein. Geneva: Droz, 1969.

Ghiberti, L. *I commentarii*, ed. L. Bartoli. Florence: Giunti, 1998.

Hotman, F. *De legibus populi romani*. Basel, 1557.

Huygens, C. *Horologium Oscillatorium (The Pendulum Clock)*, tr. R. J. Blackwell. Ames: Iowa State University Press, 1986.

Jacopo da Cessole. *Volgarizzamento del libro de' costumi e degli offizii de' nobili sopra il giuoco degli scacchi*. Milan, 1829.

Kepler, J. *Hamonices Mundi*. Linz: Johannes Plancus, 1619.

Kotruljević/Cotrugli, B. *Della mercatura e del mercante perfetto*. Venice: Dall'Elefanta, 1572.

Landino, C. *Comento sopra la Comedia*, 4 vols., ed. P. Procaccioli. Rome: Salerno, 2001.

Latini, B. *Il Tesoro*. Venice: Nicolini da Sabbio, 1528.

Ligorio, P. *Libro dei pesi, delle misure e dei vasi antichi*, ed. S. Pafumi. Rome: De Luca, 2011.

Lomazzo, G. P. *Trattato dell'arte della pittura, scoltura et architettura*. Milan: P. G. Ponzio, 1585.

Lomazzo, G. P. *Idea del tempio della pittura*. Milan: P. G. Ponzio, 1590.

Manetti, A. *Vita di Filippo Brunelleschi*, ed. D. de Robertis. Milan: Il Polifilo, 1976.

Massaria D. *De Ponderibus et mensuris medicinalibus*. Zurich: Froschover, 1584.

Mauro, L. *Le antichità de la città di Roma*. Venice: Giordano Ziletti, 1556.

Mexía, P. *La Selva di Varia Lettione*, tr. M. Roseo. Venice: Michele Tramezzino, 1547.

Mouton, G. *Observationes diametrorum solis et lunae apparentium*. Lyon, 1670.

Musso, C. *Il primo libro delle prediche*. Venice: Gabriel Giolitto de' Ferrari, 1567.

Muzio, G. *Avvertimenti morali*. Venice, 1550.

Muzio, G. *Il gentilhuomo*. Venice: Valvassori, 1571.

Muzio, G. *Battaglia in difesa dell'italica lingua*. Venice: Pietro Dusinelli, 1582.

Nesi, P. *Orationi diverse, et nuove di eccellentissimi autori*. Florence: Doni, 1547.

Nicholas of Cusa. *The Layman on Wisdom and the Mind*, tr. M. L. Führer. Ottawa: Dovehouse Editions, 1989.

*Novellae*, ed. Rudolf Schöll and Wilhelm Kroll, vol. 3 of *Corpus iuris civilis*. Berlin: Weidmann, 1895.

Osório, J. *De Rebus Emmanuelis Regis Lusitaniae Invictissimi Virtute et Auspicio Gestis*. Lisbon, 1571.

Pacioli, L. *Summa de arithmetica, geometria, proportioni et proportionalita*. Venice: Paganini, 1494.

Pacioli, L. *Divina Proportione*. Venice: Paganini, 1509.

Palladio, A. *I quattro libri dell'architettura*. Venice: Dominico de' Franceschi, 1570.

Paolo da Certaldo, *Libro di buoni costumi*, ed. A. Schiaffini. Florence: Le Monnier, 1945.

Peto, L. *De mensuris et ponderibus Romanis et Graecis*. Venice: Aldo Manuzio, 1573.

Philandrier, G. *In decem libros M. Vitruuii Pollionis de architectura annotationes*. Rome: G. A. Dossena, 1544.

Piccolomini, A. *La sfera del mondo*, Venice: Varisco and Paganini, 1566.

Pico della Mirandola, G. *La dignità dell'uomo*, ed. R. Ebgi. Turin. Einaudi: 2021.

Piero della Francesca. *De prospectiva pingendi*, ed. C. Gizzi. Venice: Ca' Foscari, 2016.

*Polibio historico greco tradotto per m. Lodovico Domenichi*. Venice: Gabriel Giolito de Ferrari, 1545.

Poliziano, A. Epistle to Franciotto Orsini. In *Opera Omnia*. Lyon: Seb. Gryphium, 1533, pp. 145–46.

Porzio, L. *De sestertio, pecuniis, ponderibus et mensuris antiquis*, 1514.

Priuli, G. *I diarii*. In *Rerum Italicorum Scriptores*, series 2 (Carducci-Fiorini ed.), vol. 24, part 3. Bologna, 1912–38.

Regiomontanus, Oratio Iohannis de Monteregio, habita in Patavii. In *Opera collectanea*, ed. F. Schmeidler. Osnabrück: Zeller, 1972, pp. 43–53.

Reisch, G. *Margarita philosophica*. Strasbourg: Johannes Grüninger, 1512.

*Relazioni sul governo della Toscana*, ed. A. Salvestrini. Florence: Olschki, 1969.

Savonarola, G. *Prediche sopra Iob*. Venice: Niccolò Bascarini, 1545.

Scaruffi, G. *L'Altinonfo*. Reggio Emilia, 1582.

Serlio, S. *Il terzo libro*. Venice: Marcolini, 1540.

Stevin, S. *De Thiende*. Leiden: Christoffel Plantijn, 1585.

*Statuta populi et communis Florentiae*. Freiburg: Kluch, 1778.

*Statuti di Volterra I (1210–1224)*, ed. E. Fiumi. Siena: Tipografia nuova, 1951.

*Statuto dell'Arte della lana di Firenze (1317–1319)*, ed. A. M. E. Agnoletti. Florence: Le Monnier, 1940.

*Statuto del podestà del 1325*, ed. R. Caggese, vol. 2 of *Statuti della Repubblica Fiorentina*. Florence: Ariani, 1910–21.

Tartaglia, N. *Nova Scientia*. Venice: Da Sabio, 1537.

Tartaglia, N. *General trattato di numeri, et misure*. Venice: Curzio Troiano Navò, 1560.

*Tavole di ragguaglio per la riduzione di pesi e misure che si usano in diversi luoghi del Granducato di Toscana al peso e misura vegliante in Firenze*. Florence, 1782.

*Tavole di ragguaglio dei pesi e delle misure … col metro decimale*. Rome. Stamperia Reale, 1877.

*Tavole di riduzione delle misure e pesi toscani alle misure e pesi analoghi del nuovo sistema metrico dell'impero francese*. Florence: Molini, Landi and Company, 1809.

Ubaldini, F. (1969). *Vita di di Mons. Angelo Colocci, edizione del testo originale italiano, Barb. Lat. 4882*, ed. V. Fanelli. Vatican City: Biblioteca apostolica Vaticana.

Varchi, B. *La prima parte delle Lezzioni*. Florence: Giunti, 1560.

Vasari, G. *Vite de' più eccellenti pittori, scultori e architettori*, ed. G. Milanesi. Florence: Sansoni, 1878–85.

Vico, E. *Discorsi sopra la medaglie degli antichi*. Venice: Giolitto de' Ferrari, 1558.

Viggiani dal Montone, A. *Lo schermo*. Venice: Angelieri, 1575.

Villani, G. *Nuova Chronica*, ed. G. Porta. Parma: Guanda, 1991.

Ximenes, L. *Del vecchio e nuovo gnomone fiorentino e delle osservazioni astronomiche, fisiche ed architettoniche fatte nel verificarne la costruzione*. Florence: Stamperia imperiale, 1757.

## Secondary Sources

Accame Lanzillota, M. (1986). *Leonardo Bruni traduttore di Demostene: la "Pro Ctesiphonte."* Genoa: Istituto nazionale di filologia classica e medievale.

Aiken, J. (1980). Leon Battista Alberti's System of Human Proportions. *Journal of the Warburg and Courtauld Institutes* 43: 68–96.

Alder K. (2002). *The Measure of All Things: The Seven-Year Odyssey and Hidden Error that Transformed the World*. New York: Free Press.

Ames-Lewis, F. (2000). *The Intellectual Life of the Early Renaissance Artist*. New Haven, CT: Yale University Press.

Ascani, V. (1997). *Il Trecento disegnato. Le basi progettuali dell'architettura gotica in Italia*. Rome: Viella.

Atwell, A. (2006). Ritual Trading: Florentine Wool-Cloth Botteghe. In R. J. Crum and J. T. Paoletti, eds., *Renaissance Florence: A Social History*. Cambridge: Cambridge University Press, pp. 182–215.

Bacci, M. (2000). *"Pro remedio anmae": Immagini sacre e pratiche devozionali in Italia centrale (secoli XIII e XIV)*. Pisa: ETS.

Bacci, M. (2014). *The Many Faces of Christ*. London: Reaktion.

Baird, D. (2004). *Thing Knowledge: A Philosophy of Scientific Instruments*. Berkeley: University of California Press.

Baldini, G. (1989). L'oscuro linguaggio del Tempio di S. Sebastiano in Mantova. *Mitteilungen des Kunsthistorischen Institutes in Florenz* 33: 155–204.

Barkan, L. (1999). *Unearthing the Past: Archaeology and Aesthetics in the Making of Renaissance Culture*. New Haven, CT: Yale University Press.

Barker, S. (2022). Cosimo I de' Medici and the Renaissance Sciences: "To Measure and to See." In A. Assonitis and H. T. Van Veen, eds., *A Companion to Cosimo I de' Medici*. Leiden: Brill, pp. 520–80.

Baslez, M. F. (2005). The Author of Wisdom and the Cultural Environment of Alexandria. In A. Passaro and G. Bellia, eds., *The Book of Wisdom in Modern Research*. Berlin: De Gruyter, pp. 33–52.

Baxandall, M. (1972). *Painting and Experience in Fifteenth-Century Italy*. Oxford: Oxford University Press.

Beck, U. (2010). Klima des Wandels oder Wie wird die grüne Moderne möglich? In H. Welzer, H.-G. Soeffner, and D. Giesecke, eds., *KlimaKulturen. Soziale Wirklichkeiten im Klimawandel*. Frankfurt: Campus, pp. 33–48.

Beeley, P. and Scriba, C. J. (2012). *Correspondence of John Wallis. Volume III (October 1558–1671)*. Oxford: Oxford University Press.

Belting, H. (2011). *Florence and Baghdad: Renaissance Art and Arab Science*. Cambridge, MA: Belknap Press.

Bennett, J. (2011). Early Modern Mathematical Instruments. *Isis* 102: 697–705.

Bensoussan, D. (2019). Casting a New Rome. PhD Dissertation, Yale University.

Bernardi, M. (2017). Colocci e Tebaldeo di fronte al Sacco di Roma (1527): le liste *fege* un nuovo documento epistolare. *Miscellanea bibliothecae apostolicae vaticanae* 23: 35–118.

Bertelli, C. (1991). *Piero della Francesca*. Milan: Silvana.

Biagioli, M. (1993). *Galileo, Courtier*. Chicago, IL: University of Chicago Press.

Bianchi, L. (2009). Per una storia dell'Aristotelismo 'volgare' nel Rinascimento. *Bruniana & Campanelliana* 15(2): 367–85.

Bianchi Giovini, A. (1865). *Le Prediche domenicali*. Milan: Francesco Sanvito.

Bione, C. (1910). I più antichi trattati di arte retorica. *Annali della R. Scuola Nomale Superiore* 22: 3–157.

Black, J. (2005). *European Warfare, 1494–1660*. London: Taylor & Francis.

Black. R. (2007). *Education and Society in Florentine Tuscany: Teachers, Pupils and Schools, c. 1250–1500*. Leiden: Brill.

Bognolo, A. (2012). Nel labirinto della Selva. La traduzione italiana della *Silva de varia lección* di Mambrino Roseo da Fabriano. In V. Nider, ed., *Il prisma di Proteo*. Trento: University of Trento, pp. 257–306.

Bolognesi, D. (2007). Libertà e privilegi del mercato. I sensali a Ravenna in età moderna. *I Quaderni del Cardello* 17: 263–98.

Bork, R. (2016). *The Geometry of Creation*. New York: Routledge.

Borlandi, A. (1963). *Il Manuale di Mercatura di Saminiato de' Ricci*. Genoa: Di Stefano.

Borsi, F. (1980). *Leon Battista Alberti: L'opera completa*. Milan: Electa.

Bortolozzi, A. (2020). *Italian Architectural Drawings*. Berlin: Hatje Cantz Verlag GmbH.

Bredekamp, H. (2019). *Galileo's Thinking Hand: Mannerism, Anti-mannerism, and the Virtue of Drawing in the Foundation of Early Modern Science*. Berlin: De Gruyter.

Brothers, C. (2021). *Giuliano da Sangallo and the Ruins of Rome*. Princeton, NJ: Princeton University Press.

Brown, J. (2020). Language History from Below: Standardization and Koineization in Renaissance Italy. *Journal of Historical Sociolinguistics* 6 (1): 1–28.

Bruschi, A. (2004). *L'Antico, la tradizione, il moderno: da Arnolfo a Peruzzi*. Milan: Electa.

Burckhardt, J. (1890). *The Civilisation of the Renaissance in Italy*, tr. S. G. C. Middlemore. New York: Macmillan.

Burke, P. (1997). *The Renaissance*. Houndsmill: Palgrave Macmillan.

Burnett, A. (2017). Budé's *Breviarium*: Authorship, Date, and Purpose. *Journal of the Warburg and Courtauld Institutes* 80: 101–26.

Busard, H. L. (1965). The Practica Geometriae of Dominicus de Clavasio. *Archive for History of Exact Sciences* 2(6): 520–75.

Caciagli, C. (1978). Considerazioni sul braccio volterrano. *Volterra* 17(12): 4–7.

Camerota, F. (2004). *Il compasso geometrico e militare di Galileo Galilei*. Florence: Istituto e Museo della Scienza.

Camerota, F. (2006). Teaching Euclid in a Practical Context: Linear Perspective and Practical Geometry. *Science & Education* 15: 323–34.

Camerota, F. (2015). Le regole del disegno prospettico. In F. Camerota, F. P. Di Teodoro, and L. Grasselli, eds., *Piero della Francesca: Il disegno tra arte e scienza*. Milan: Skira, pp. 39–51.

Camerota, F. (2016). I Sei libri di Prospettiva di Vincenzo Scamozzi. In F. Barbieri, M. E. Avagnina, and P. Sanvito, eds., *Vincenzo Scamozzi teorico europeo*. Vicenza: Accademia Olimpica, pp. 18–39.

Cantile, A. (2005). Misura e rappresentazione urbana nelle opere di Leon Battista Alberti. In R. Cardini, ed., *Leon Battista Alberti: la biblioteca di un umanista*. Florence: Mandragora, pp. 121–26.

Carlà, F. (2009). *L'oro nella tarda antichità: aspetti economici e sociali*. Turin: Silvio Zamorani.

Carlton, G. (2015). *Worldly Consumers: The Demand for Maps in Renaissance Italy*. Chicago, IL: University of Chicago Press.

Carpo, M. (2001). *Architecture in the Age of Printing: Orality, Writing, Typography, and Printed Images in the History of Architectural Theory*. Cambridge, MA: MIT Press.

Carpo, M. and Furlan, F. (2007). Introduction. In L. B. Alberti, *Delineation of the City of Rome*. Tempe, AZ: Center for Medieval and Renaissance Texts and Studies, pp. 3–18.

Carrera Stampa, M. (1949). The Evolution of Weights and Measures in New Spain. *Hispanic American Historical Review* 29(1): 2–24.

Casamassima, E. and Rubinstein, R. (1993) *Antiquarian Drawings from Dosio's Roman Workshop*. Milan: Giunta regionale toscana.

Casper, A. R. (2021). *An Artful Relic: The Shroud of Turin in Baroque Italy*. University Park, Pennsylvania State University Press.

Cassirer, E. (1963). *The Individual and the Cosmos in Renaissance Philosophy*. Oxford: Blackwell.

Castano Musicò, L. (1990). Il commento di Angelo Poliziano alle Georgiche di Virgilio. *Materiali e discussioni per l'analisi dei testi classici* 24: 181–90.

Castelli, P. (1987). Il moto aristotelico e la "licita scientia." In P. Castelli, M. Mingardi, and M. Padovan, eds., *Mesura et arte del danzare*. Pesaro: Comune, pp. 35–57.

Cattaneo, A. (2011). Map Projections and Perspective in the Renaissance. In Z. Shalev and C. Burnett, eds., *Ptolemy's "Geography" in the Renaissance*. London: Warburg Institute, pp. 51–80.

Cavallar, O. (2004). River of Law: Bartolus' s Tiberiadis (De alluvione). In J. A. Marino and T. Kuehn, eds., *A Renaissance of Conflicts: Visions and Revisions of Law and Society in Italy and Spain*. Toronto: Centre for Reformation and Renaissance Studies, pp. 31–131.

Cazals, G. (2008). *Une civile société: la République selon Guillaume de la Perrière*. Toulouse: Presses de l'Université des sciences sociales.

Chiavari, A. (1981). Misure agrimensorie altomedievali dell'Italia centrale: il piede di Liutprando ed il moggio nell'area marchigiana nei secoli VIII–XII. *Atti e Memorie della Deputazione di Storia Patria per le Marche* 86: 895–953.

Christian, W. A. (1981). *Local Religion in Sixteenth-Century Spain*. Princeton, NJ: Princeton University Press.

Ciapponi, L. A. (1960). Il "De architectura" di Vitruvio nel primo umanesimo." *Italia medioevale e umanistica* 3: 59–99.

Ciocci, A. (2016). Luca Pacioli e l'uomo vitruviano nel Rinascimento. In M. Martelli, ed., *Luca Pacioli e i grandi artisti del Rinascimento italiano*. Sansepolcro: Centro studi Mario Pancrazi, pp. 121–64.

Cipolla, C. M. (1989). *Money in Sixteenth-Century Florence*. Berkeley: University of California Press.

Clarke, G. (2002). Vitruvian Paradigms. *Papers of the British School at Rome* 70: 319–46.

Conway, M. (1999). *The* Diario *of the Printing Press of San Jacopo di Ripoli, 1476–1484*. Florence: Olschki.

Cox, V. (2016). *A Short History of the Italian Renaissance*. London: Tauris.

Crease, R. P. (2011). *World in the Balance: The Historic Quest for an Absolute System of Measurement*. New York: W. W. Norton.

Cremona, J. (1997). "Acciocch'ognuno le possa intendere": The Use of Italian As a Lingua Franca on the Barbary Coast of the Seventeenth Century. *Journal of Anglo-Italian Studies* 5: 52–69.

Crosby, A. W. (1988). *The Measure of Reality: Quantification in Western Society, 1250–1600*. Cambridge: Cambridge University Press.

Cuomo, S. (2000). Divide and Rule: Frontinus and Roman Land-Surveying. *Studies in History and Philosophy of Science* 31(2): 189–202.

Curran, B. and Grafton, A. (1995). A Fifteenth-Century Site Report on the Vatican Obelisk. *Journal of the Warburg and Courtauld Institutes* 58: 234–48.

Currie, E. (2009). Fashion Networks: Consumer Demand and the Clothing Trade in Florence from the Mid-Sixteenth to Early Seventeenth Centuries. *Journal of Medieval and Early Modern Studies* 39(3): 483–509.

Dacos, N. (1989). Le rôle des plaquettes dans la diffusion des gemmes antiques: le cas de la collection Médicis. *Studies in the History of Art* 22: 71–91.

Damisch, H. (1994). *The Origin of Perspective*. Cambridge, MA: MIT Press.

Damisch, H. (2002). *A Theory of /Cloud/: Towards a History of Painting*. Stanford, CA: Stanford University Press.

Daston, L. and Galison, P. (2007). *Objectivity*. Boston, MA: MIT Press.

Davies, K. (1985). Leonardo Porzio in the 1527 De Asse. *Acta conventus neolatini Bononiensis*. Binghamton: Center for Medieval and Early Renaissance Studies, pp. 430–46.

De Lubac, H. (1959–64). *Exégèse medievale: les quatre sens de l'écriture*. Paris: Aubier.

De Luca, G. (2010). Sensali e mercato del credito a Milano tra 16. e 17. Secolo. In E. M. García Guerra and G. De Luca, eds. *Il mercato del credito in età moderna. Reti e operatori finanziari nello spazio europeo*. Milan: FrancoAngeli, pp. 239–57.

Del Re, N. (1986). Luca Peto giureconsulto e magistrato capitolino (1512–1580). In *Scritti in onore di Filippo Caraffa*. Anagni: Istituto di Storia e di Arte del Lazio Meridionale, pp. 309–37.

D'Onofrio. C. (1968). *Il Tevere e Roma*. Rome: Bozzi.

De Rusysscher, D. (2018). How Normative Were Merchant Guidebooks? In H. Pihlajamäki, A. Cordes, S. Dauchy, and D. de Ruysscher, eds., *Understanding the Sources of Early Modern and Modern Commercial Law*. Leiden: Brill, pp. 144–65.

De Sanctis, G. (1970). *Scritti minori*. 6 vols. Vol. 2. Rome: Edizioni di storia e letteratura.

Delaruelle, L. (1907). *Guillaume Budé: les origines, les débuts, les idées maîtresses*. Paris: Champion.

Didi-Huberman, G. (1998). The Portrait, the Individual and the Singular: Remarks on the Legacy of Aby Warburg. In N. Mann and L. Syson, eds., *The Image of the Individual: Portraits in the Renaissance*. London: British Museum, pp. 165–88.

Dijkman, J. (2011). *Shaping Medieval Markets: The Organisation of Commodity Markets in Holland, c. 1200–c. 1450*. Leiden: Brill.

Di Pasquale, S. (2001). *L'arte del costruire*. Venice: Marsilio.

Di Teodoro, F. P. (1994). *Raffaello, Baldassar Castiglione e la 'Lettera a Leone X.* Bologna: Nuova Alfa.

Docci, M. (1987). I rilievi di Leonardo da Vinci per la redazione della pianta di Imola. *Quaderni dell'Istituto di Storia dell'Architettura* 1(10): 181–86.

Drake S. (1986). Galileo's Physical Measurements. *American Journal of Physics* 54(4): 302–06.

Ducos, M. (2002). Legal Science in France in the 16–17th centuries. In G. Sandy, ed., *The Classical Heritage in France.* Leiden: Brill, pp. 297–314.

Dunlop, J. (2012). What Geometry Postulates. In A. Janiak and E. Schliesser, eds., *Interpreting Newton: Critical Essays.* Cambridge: Cambridge University Press, pp. 69–101.

Eco, U. (2022). *Sulle spalle dei giganti.* Milan: Bompiani.

Edelheit, A. (2008). *Ficino, Pico and Savonarola: The Evolution of Humanist Theology 1461/2–1498.* Leiden: Brill.

Edgerton, S. (1974). Florentine Interests in Ptolemaic Cartography As Background for Renaissance Painting, Architecture, and the Discovery of America. *Journal of the Society of Architectural Historians* 33: 274–92.

Elden, S. (2013). *The Birth of the Territory.* Chicago, IL: University of Chicago Press.

Elkins, J. (1994). *The Poetics of Perspective.* Ithaca, NY: Cornell University Press.

Engammare, M. (2013). Glarean's Bible. In I. Fenlon and I. M. Groote, eds., *Heinrich Glarean's Books: The Intellectual World of a Sixteenth-Century Musical Humanist.* Cambridge: Cambridge University Press, pp. 91–109.

Epstein, S. R. (2000). *Freedom and Growth: The Rise of States and Markets in Europe (1300–1750).* New York: Routledge.

Eran, A. (1986). Samen in der Metrologie. In H. Witthöft, ed., *Die historische Metrologie in den Wissenschaften.* St. Katharinen: Scripta Mercaturae, pp. 248–61.

Fane-Saunders, P. (2016). *Pliny the Elder and the Emergence of Renaissance Architecture.* Cambridge: Cambridge University Press.

Fanelli, V. (1979). Aspetti della Roma cinquecentesca. Le case e le raccolte archeologiche del Colocci. In V. Fanelli, ed., *Ricerche su Angelo Colocci e sulla Roma cinquecentesca.* Vatican City: Biblioteca Apostolica Vaticana, pp. 111–25.

Favaro. A. (1901). *Il metro proposto come unità di misura nel 1675.* Mâcon: Protat.

Federici Vescovini, G. (1965). Contributo per la storia della fortuna di Alhazen in Italia: il volgarizzamento del MS Vat. 4595 e il 'Commentario Terzo' del Ghiberti. *Rinascimento* 5: 17–49.

Fedreghini, G. G. (1752). *Ricerca del piede statutario di Brescia.* Brescia: G. Bossino.

Fend, M. (2019). Drawing the Cadaver ad vivum: Gérard de Lairesse's Illustrations for Govard Bidloo's Anatomia Humani Corporis. In T. Balfe, J. Woodall, and C. Zittel, eds., *Ad Vivum? Visual Materials and the Vocabulary of Life-Likeness in Europe before 1800.* Leiden: Brill, pp. 294–327.

Filippi, E. (2008). "Halt Mass": Attieniti alla misura! Dürer e la proportizione nelle cose. *Atti e memorie dell'Accademia Toscana di Scienze e Lettere "La Colombaria."* 59: 39–61.

Filippi, G. (1889). *L'Arte dei mercanti di Calimala in Firenze e il suo più antico statuto.* Turin: Bocca.

Finiello Zervas, D. (1979). The Florentine Braccio da Panna. *Architectura* 9: 6–10.

Fiocca, A. (1998). *Giambattista Aleotti e Ali ingegneri del rinascimento.* Florence: L. S. Olshki.

Fiorini, A. (2015). Modani e campioni mensori: verso un censimento dell'Italia centro-settentrionale (secoli XIII–XVIII). *Debates de Arqueología Medieval* 5: 69–90.

Frangioni, L. (1992). *Milano e le sue misure: Appunti di metrologia lombarda fra Tre e Quattrocento.* Naples: Edizioni scientifiche italiane.

Freiberg, J. (2014). *Bramante's Tempietto, the Roman Renaissance, and the Spanish Crown.* Cambridge: Cambridge University Press.

Fricke, B. (2015). *Fallen Idols, Risen Saints: Sainte Foy of Conques and the Revival of Monumental Sculpture in Medieval Art.* Turnhout: Brepols.

Frojmovič, E. (1996). Giotto's Allegories of Justice and the Commune in the Palazzo della Ragione in Padua. *Journal of the Warburg and Courtauld Institutes* 59, 24–47.

Frommel, C. L. (1994). *The Architectural Drawings of Antonio da Sangallo the Younger and His Circle.* Cambridge, Mass. MIT Press.

Frommel, C. L. (1998). Francesco dal Borgo e la tradizione Michelozziana. In G. Morolli, ed., *Michelozzo, scultore e architetto (1396–1472).* Florence: CentroDi, pp. 257–62.

Frommel, C. L. (2008). Formazione e evoluzione architettonica di Andrea Bregno. In C. Crescentini and C. Strinati, eds., *Andrea Bregno: il senso della forma nella cultura artistica del Rinascimento.* Florence: Maschietto, 2008, pp. 171–97.

Gadoffre, G. (1997). *La révolution culturelle dans la France des humanistes.* Geneva: Droz.

Galletto, D. and Barberis, B. (2006). Lagrange e le origini della Méchanique analitique. In G. Sacchi Landriani and A. Giorgilli, eds., *Sfogliando la Méchanique analitique.* Milan: LED, pp. 77–108.

Garin, E. (1986). *L'Umanesimo italiano: filosofia e vita civile nel Rinascimento*. Rome: Laterza.

Gasparotto, D. (1996). Ricerche sull'antica metrologia tra Cinque e Seicento: Pirro Ligorio e Nicolas-Claude Fabri de Peiresc. *Annali della Scuola Normale Superiore di Pisa. Classe di Lettere e Filosofia* 1(1): 279–324.

Gautier Dalché, P. (2009). *La Géographie de Ptolémée en Occident (IVe–XIVe siècle)*. Turnhout: Brepols.

Giráldéz, A. (2019). Money and Its Technologies. In S. Deng, ed., *A Cultural History of Money in the Renaissance*. London: Bloomsbury, pp. 15–38.

Giuliani, M. (2006). *Le arti fiorentine*. Florence: Scramasax.

Goldthwaite, R. A. (1975). I prezzi del grano a Firenze dal XIV al XVI secolo. *Quaderni storici* 10(28): 5–36.

Goldthwaite, R. A. (2008). *The Economy of Renaissance Florence*. Baltimore, MD: Johns Hopkins University Press.

Gombrich, E. H. (1961). Renaissance and Golden Age. *Journal of the Warburg and Courtauld Institutes* 24(3/4): 306–09.

Gregory, A. (2022). Mathematics and Cosmology in Plato's *Timaeus. Apeiron* 55(3): 359–89.

Grendler, P. F. (2004). *The Universities of the Italian Renaissance*. Baltimore, MD: Johns Hopkins University Press.

Grierson, P. (1975). *Numismatics*. Oxford: Oxford University Press.

Guarducci A. (2009). *L'utopia del catasto nella Toscana di Pietro Leopoldo*. Borgo San Lorenzo: All'insegna del giglio.

Guarducci, M. (1983). *Scritti scelti sulla religione greco e romana e sul cristianesimo*. Leiden: Brill.

Guasti, C. (1887). *Santa Maria del Fiore; la costruzione della Chiesa e del campanile secondo i documenti*. Florence: Ricci.

Gueudet, G. (1968). Une lettre inédite de Budé à Alciat. *Moreana* 19/20: 70–90.

Guidoni, E. (1989). *Il Duecento*. Rome: Laterza.

Günther, H. (1981/82). Die Rekonstruktion des antiken römischen Fußmaßes in der Renaissance. *Sitzungsberichte der Kunstgeschichtlichen Gesellschaft zu Berlin* 30: 8–12.

Günther, H. (1988). *Das Studium der antiken Architektur in den Zeichnungen der Hochrenaissance*. Tübingen. Ernst Wasmuth.

Günther, H. (1989). Serlio e gli ordini architettonici. In C. Thoenes, ed., *Sebastiano Serlio*. Milan: Electa, pp. 154–68.

Hadot, P. (2006). *The Veil of Isis*. Cambridge, MA: Belknap Press.

Hallyn, F. (2008). *Gemma Frisius, arpenteur de la terre et du ciel*. Paris: Champion.

Hankins, J. (1992). Ptolemy's Geography in the Renaissance. In R. G. Dennis and E. Falsey, eds., *The Marks in the Fields*. Cambridge, MA: Harvard University Press, pp. 119–27.

Harreld, D. J. (2010) Foreign Merchants and International Trade Networks in the Sixteenth-Century Low Countries. *Journal of European Economic History* 39(1): 11–31.

Harris, J. (1994). *The Palladian Revival: Lord Burlington, His Villa and Garden at Chiswick*. New Haven, CT: Yale University Press.

Haskell, F. and Penny, N. (1981). *Taste and the Antique: The Lure of Classical Sculpture, 1500–1900*. New Haven, CT: Yale University Press.

Hasse, D. N. (2021) Three Double Translations from Arabic into Latin by Gerard of Cremona and Dominicus Guindisalvi. In D. Calma, ed., *Reading Proclus and the Books of Causes*. Leiden: Brill, pp. 247–74.

Heilbron, J. L. (1990). Introduction. In J. L. Heilbron, ed., *The Quantifying Spirit in the Eighteenth Century*. Los Angeles: University of California Press, pp. 1–24.

Heilbron, J. L. (2000). *Geometry Civilized: History, Culture, and Technique*. Oxford: Clarendon.

Hendrix, J. (2011). *Leon Battista Alberti and the Concept of Lineament*. Conference proceeding. https://docs.rwu.edu/saahp_fp/30.

Hendrix, J. (2017). Renaissance Aesthetics and Mathematics. In I. Alexander-Skipnes, ed., *Visual Culture and Mathematics in the Early Modern Period*. New York: Routledge, pp. 11–31.

Henschel, K. A. (1855). *Das bequemste Maas- und Gewichts-System gegründet auf den natürlichen Schritt des Menschen*. Kassel: Betram.

Herselle Krinsky, C. (1967). Seventy-Eight Vitruvius Manuscripts. *Journal of the Warburg and Courtauld Institutes* 30: 36–70.

Heseler, B. (1959). *Andreas Vesalius' First Public Anatomy at Bologna, 1540*. Uppsala: Almqvist & Wiksells.

Hoock, J. and Jeannin, P. (1991). *Ars Mercatoria: Handbücher und Traktate für den Gebrauch des Kaufmanns*. Paderborn: Schöningh.

Høyrup, J. (1994). *In Measure, Number, and Weight: Studies in Mathematics and Culture*. Albany: State University of New York Press.

Hülsen, C. (1884). Sopra un edifizio antico esistente presso la chiesa di S. Adriano al Foro Romano. *Annali dell'istituto di corrispondenza archeologica* 56: 323–56.

Hunt, E. S. (1994). *The Medieval Super-Companies: A Study of the Peruzzi Company of Florence*. Cambridge: Cambridge University Press.

Inalcik, H. (1983). Introduction to Ottoman Metrology. *Turcica: Revue d'études turques* 15: 311–48.

Jaquet, D., Verelst, K., and Dawson T., eds. (2015). *Late Medieval and Early Modern Fight Books: Transmission and Tradition of Martial Arts in Europe (14th–17th Centuries)*. Leiden: Brill.

Jesseph, D. (1993). Of Analytics and Indivisibles: Hobbes on the Methods of Modern Mathematics. *Revue d'histoire des sciences* 46(2): 153–93.

Joost-Gaugier, C. L. (2006). *Measuring Heaven: Pythagoras and His Influence on Thought and Art in Antiquity and the Middle Ages*. Ithaca, NY: Cornell University Press.

Kedar, B. Z. (1976). *Merchants in Crisis, Genoese and Venetian Men of Affairs and the Fourteenth-Century Depression*. New Haven, CT: Yale University Press.

Kelly, D. (1988). Jurisconsultus Perfectus: The Lawyer As Renaissance Man. *Journal of the Warburg and Courtauld Institutes* 51: 84–102.

Kemp, M. (1978). Science, Non-science and Nonsense: The Interpretation of Brunelleschi's Perspective. *Art History* 1(2): 134–61.

King, P. (2009). Emotions in Medieval Thought. In P. Goldie, ed., *Oxford Handbook on Emotion*. Oxford: Oxford University Press, pp. 167–88.

Kren, T. (2018). *Christian Imagery and the Development of the Nude in Europe*. In T. Kren, ed., *The Renaissance Nude*. Los Angeles: Getty Institute, pp. 17–79.

Kuhn, J. R. (1990). Measured Appearances: Documentation and Design in Early Perspective Drawing. *Journal of the Warburg and Courtauld Institutes* 53: 114–32.

Kula, W. (1986). *Men and Measures*. Princeton, NJ: Princeton University Press.

Kusukawa, S. (2012). *Picturing the Book of Nature: Image, Text, and Argument in Sixteenth-Century Human Anatomy and Medical Botany*. Chicago, IL: University of Chicago Press.

La Rocca, E. and Parisi Presicce, C. (2010). *Musei capitolini*, vol. 1: *Le sculture del Palazzo Nuovo*. Milan: Electa.

Lattès, S. (1972). A proposito dell'opera incompiuta "De ponderibus et mensuris" di Angelo Colocci. *Atti del Convegno di studi su Angelo Colocci*. Jesi: Comune, pp. 97–108.

Laudan, L. (1981). *Science and Hypothesis*. Dordrecht: Reidel.

Le Goff, J. (2015). *Must We Divide History into Periods?* New York: Columbia University Press.

Leftwich, G. V. (1995). Polykleitos and Hippokratic Medicine. In W. G. Moon, ed., *Polykleitos, the Doryphoros, and Tradition*. Madison: University of Wisconsin Press, pp. 38–51.

Lemerle, F. (1994). Philandrier et le texte de Viutruve. *Mélanges de l'école française de Rome* 106(2): 517–29.

LeNotre, G. G. (2016). Thomas Aquinas and the Method of Predication in Metaphysics. PhD dissertation. Catholic University of America.

Lepenies, P. (2014). *Art, Politics, and Development: How Linear Perspective Shaped Policies in the Western World*. Philadelphia, PA: Temple University Press.

Lewis, M. J. T. (2001). *Surveying Instruments of Greece and Rome*. Cambridge: Cambridge University Press.

Lincoln, E. (2014). *Brilliant Discourse: Pictures and Readers in Early Modern Rome*. New Haven, CT: Yale University Press.

Lindberg, D. C. (1976). *Theories of Vision from Al-Kindi to Kepler*. Chicago, IL: University of Chicago Press.

Liva, G. (2008). Il collegio degli ingegneri architetti e agrimensori di Milano. In G. Bigatti and M. Canella, eds., *Il Collegio degli ingegneri e architetti di Milano*. Milan: FrancoAngeli.

Long, P. O. (2018) *Engineering the Eternal City*. Chicago, IL: University of Chicago Press.

Lopez, R. (1955). *Medieval Trade in the Mediterranean World*. New York: Columbia University Press.

Lugli, E. (2019a). *The Making of Measure and the Promise of Sameness*. Chicago, IL: University of Chicago Press.

Lugli, E. (2019b). In cerca della perfezione: nuovi elementi per l'Uomo vitruviano di Leonardo Da Vinci. In F. Borgo, ed., *Leonardo e Vitruvio*. Venice, Marsilio, pp. 69–91.

Mac Carthy, I. (2020). *The Grace of the Italian Renaissance*. Princeton, NJ: Princeton University Press.

Maetzke, G. (1990). La chiesa di S. Salvatore de' Stadera al Foro Romano. *Archeologia laziale* 10: 98–104.

Maier, J. (2015). *Rome Measured and Imagined*. Chicago, IL: University of Chicago Press.

Magni, S. (2015). Politica degli approvvigionamenti e controllo del commercio dei cereali nell'Italia dei comuni nel XIII e XIV secolo: alcune questioni preliminari. *Mélanges de l'École Française de Rome* 127 (1). https://doi.org/10.4000/mefrm.2473.

Mangani, G. (2018). *La bellezza del numero: Angelo Colocci e le origini dello stato nazione*. Ancona: Lavoro editoriale.

Maniura, R. (2009). Ex Votos, Art and Pious Performance. *Oxford Art Journal* 32(3): 409–25.

Manni, D. M. (alias Tubalco Panichio) (1734). Del Piede Aliprando e del piede della Porta. *Raccolta d'opuscoli di A. Calogera* 10: 125–83.

Manni, D. M. (1739–86). *Osservazioni istoriche sopra i sigilli antichi de' secoli bassi*. 30 vols. Florence: Albizzini.

Marani, P. C. (2009). L'Uomo vitruviano come canone per una scultura perfetta? In A. P. Torrini, ed., *Leonardo: L'uomo vitruviano fra arte e scienza*. Venice: Marsilio, pp. 99–109.

Marchard, E. (2010). Plaster and Plaster Casts in Renaissance Italy. In R. Frederiksen and E. Marchand, eds., *Plaster Cast: Making, Collecting and Displaying from Classical Antiquity to the Present*. New York: De Gruyter, pp. 49–79.

Mariani, G. (2022). *Roberto Caracciolo da Lecce (1425–1495)*. Leiden: Brill.

Marina A. (2006). Order and Ideal Geometry in the Piazza Del Duomo, Parma. *Journal of the Society of Architectural Historians* 65(4): 520–49.

Marinelli, S. (1981). The Author of the Codex Huygens. *Journal of the Warburg and Courtauld Institutes* 44: 214–20.

Martens, M. (1952). La correspondance de caractère économique échangée par Francesco Sforza, duc de milan, et Philippe le Bon, duc de Bourgogne (1450–1466). *Bulletin de l'Institut historique belge de Rome* 27: 221–34.

Massey, L. (2007). *Picturing Space, Displacing Bodies: Anamorphosis in Early Modern Theories of Perspective*. University Park: Pennsylvania State University Press.

Mattone, A. and Olivari. T. (2009). Il manuale nelle università italiane del Cinquecento: diritto e medicina. In M. G. Tavoni and G. P. Brizzi, eds., *Dalla pecia all'e-book: libri per l'università: stampa, editoria, circolazione e lettura*. Bologna: CLUEB, pp. 217–37.

Mazzocco, A. (1982). Rome and the Humanists: The Case of Biondo Flavio. In P. A. Ramsey, ed., *Rome in the Renaissance: The City and the Myth*. Binghamton, NY: Center for Medieval & Early Renaissance Studies, pp. 183–95.

Mazzotta, G. (1993). *The Worlds of Petrarch*. Durham, NC: Duke University Press.

McIntosh, C. (2010). *Semantics and Cultural Change in the British Enlightenment*. Leiden: Brill.

McNeil, D. O. (1975). *Guillaume Budé and Humanism in the Reign of Francis I*. Geneva: Droz.

Meurer, P. H. (2007). Cartography in the German Lands, 1450–1650. In D. Woodward, ed., *The History of Cartography*. Vol. 3. Chicago: IL: University of Chicago Press, pp. 1172–1245.

Michell, J. (1993). The Origins of the Representational Theory of Measurement: Helmholtz, Hölder, and Russell. *Studies in History and Philosophy of Science* 24(2): 185–206.

Michell, J. (1997). Bertrand Russell's 1897 Critique of the Traditional Theory of Measurement. *Synthese* 110: 257–76.

Milanesi, G. (1854–56) *Documenti per la storia dell'arte senese*. Siena: Porri.

Molho, A. (1968). The Florentine Oligarchy and the *Balie* of the Late Trecento. *Speculum* 43(1): 23–51.

Mondschein, K. (2014). The Number of Motion: Camillo Agrippa's Geometrical Fencing and the Enumeration of the Body. *Journal of the Northern Renaissance* 6. https://jnr2.hcommons.org/2015/3575.

Morel, T. (2020). *De Re Geometrica*: Writing, Drawing, and Preaching Mathematics in Early Modern Mines. *Isis* 111(1): 22–45.

Moreni, D. (1816). *Continuazione delle memorie istoriche dell'ambrosiana imperial basilica di S. Lorenzo di Firenze*. Florence: Daddi.

Morris, P. J. T. (2015). *The Matter Factory: A History of the Chemistry Laboratory*. Chicago, IL: University of Chicago Press.

Morsolin, B. (1894). *Giangiorgio Trissino: monografia d'un gentiluomo letterato nel secolo XVI*. Florence: Le Monnier.

Muecke, F. (2017). Biondo at Basel: The 1531 Froben Edition of "Roma Triumphans." *Bibliothèque d'Humanisme et Renaissance* 79(3): 625–35.

Murray Jones, P. and Olsan, L. T. (2015). Performative Rituals for Conception and Childbirth in England, 900–1500. *Bulletin of the History of Medicine* 89 (3): 406–33.

Mussolin, M. (2007). La Tribuna delle Reliquie di Michelangelo e la controfacciata di San Lorenzo a Firenze. In P. Ruschi, ed., *Michelangelo architetto a San Lorenzo*. Florence: Mandragora, pp. 183–226.

Muzzarelli, G. M. (2019). Questioni di limite: predicare la misura. *Cahiers d'études italiennes* 29. https://doi.org/10.4000/cei.5832.

Nardella, C. (1997). *Il fascino di Roma nel Medioevo: "Le meraviglie di Roma" di maestro Gregorio*. Rome: Viella.

Nesselrath, A. (2022). Ermeneutica fiorentina: il disegno di architettura come metodo di studio dell'antico nel Quattrocento. In A. R. Sartore, ed., *Roma ritrovata: disegni sconosciuti della cerchia dei Sangallo alla Biblioteca nazionale centrale di Firenze*. Florence: Biblioteca Nazionale Centrale, pp. 13–23.

Nepi Sciré, G. (1992). Studi di proporzioni. In P. C. Marani, ed., *Leonardo e Venezia*, Milan: Bompiani, pp. 214–27.

Nichols, F. M. (1986). *The Marvels of Rome*. New York: Italica.

Northcote, J. (1819). *Life of Sir Joshua Reynolds*. London: Henry Colburn.

Olariu, D. (2009). Réflexions sur l'avènement du portrait avant le XVe siècle. In D. Olariu, ed., *Le portrait individuel. Réflexions autour d'une forme de représentation*. Bern: Lang, pp. 83–101.

Onians, J. (1988). *Bearers of Meaning: The Classical Orders in Antiquity, the Middle Ages, and the Renaissance.* Princeton, NJ: Princeton University Press.

Pafumi, S. (2011). Introduzione. In P. Ligorio, ed., *Libro dei Pesi, delle misure, e dei vasi antichi.* Rome: De Luca, pp. ix–xxx.

Panofsky, E. (1940). *The Codex Huygens and Leonardo da Vinci's Art Theory.* London: Warburg Institute.

Panofsky, E. (1955). The History of the Theory of Human Proportions As a Reflection of the History of Styles. In E. Panofsky, ed., *Meaning in the Visual Arts.* New York, Doubleday Anchor Books, pp. 82–132.

Panofsky, E. (1960). *Renaissance and Renascences in Western Art.* Stockholm: Almqvist & Wiksell.

Panzanelli, R. (2008). Compelling Presence: Wax Effigies in Renaissance Florence. In R. Panzanelli, ed., *Ephemeral Bodies: Wax Sculpture and the Human Figure.* Los Angeles: Getty Research Institute, pp. 13–39.

Panzanelli Fratoni, M. A. (2020). Le prime edizioni a stampa dei trattati di Bartolo (1472–1500). In G. Crinella, ed., *Bartolo da Sassoferrato e il Trattato sulla tirannide* (2020). Sassoferrato: Istituto internazionale di Studi Piceni, pp. 59–87.

Parsons, P. W. (2016). Baldassarre Peruzzi at Saint Peter's: The American Academy Plan and Peruzzi's Model of 1521. *Memoirs of the American Academy in Rome* 61: 91–133.

Pastorino, C. (2021). The Early Modern Study of Ancient Measures in Comparative Perspective: A Preliminary Investigation. In D. Levitin and I. Maclean, eds., *The Worlds of Knowledge and the Classical Tradition in the Early Modern Age: Comparative Approaches.* Leiden: Brill, pp. 118–41.

Patrizi-Forti, F. (1869). Delle Memorie storiche di Norcia. Norcia: Micocci.

Pavlović, B. (2006). Roland's Column in Dubrovnik: His Role, His Changes and His Permanence. In A. Kremenjaš-Daničić, ed., *Orlandovi europski putevi/ Roland's European Paths.* Dubrovnik: Europski dom Dubrovnik, pp. 420–26.

Payne, A. (1999). *The Architectural Treatise in the Italian Renaissance: Architectural Invention, Ornament, and Literary Culture.* Cambridge: Cambridge University Press.

Pecchioli Vigni, M. C. (1971). Lo Statuto in Volgare Della Magistratura Fiorentina Della Grascia (a. 1379). *Archivio Storico Italiano* 129(1): 3–70.

Penrose, B. (1952). *Travel and Discovery in the Renaissance, 1420–1620.* Cambridge, MA: Harvard University Press.

Perucchi, G. (2016). Appunti antiquari medievali. L'iter romanum attribuito a Giovanni Dondi dall'Orologio. In E. Tinelli, ed., *Petrarca, l'Italia, l'Europa. Sulla varia fortuna di Petrarca.* Bari: Pagina, pp. 131–39.

Pfister, U. (2008). Craft Guilds, the Theory of the Firm, and Early Modern Proto-industry. In S. R. Epstein and M. Prak, eds., *Guilds, Innovation and the European Economy, 1400–1800*. Cambridge: Cambridge University Press, pp. 25–51.

Pinkus, A. (2014). *Sculpting Simulacra in Medieval Germany, 1250–1380*. Farnham: Ashgate.

Piotrowicz, P. (2013). L'immagine del mercante modello in *Il libro dell'arte di mercatura* di Benedetto Cotrugli. *Źródła Humanistyki Europejskiej* 6: 349–61.

Polecritti, C. L. (2000). *Preaching Peace in Renaissance Italy: Bernardino of Siena and His Audience*. Washington, DC: Catholic University of America Press.

Porro Lambertenghi, G. (1878). Lettere di Galeazzo Maria Sforza. *Archivio Storico Lombardo* 5: 637–68.

Porter, M. (2005). *Windows of the Soul: Physiognomy in European Culture 1470–1780*. Oxford: Oxford University Press.

Porter, T. (1995). *Trust in Numbers: The Pursuit of Objectivity in Science and Public Life*. Princeton, NJ: Princeton University Press.

Pötschke, D. (2002). *Stadtrecht, Roland und Pranger: zur Rechtsgeschichte von Halberstadt, Goslar, Bremen und Städten der Mark Brandenburg*. Berlin: Lukas.

Puttfarken, T. (2000). *The Discovery of Pictorial Composition: Theories of Visual Order in Painting, 1400–1800*. New Haven, CT: Yale University Press.

Quondam, A. (2021). *Il Letterato e il Pittore: Per una storia dell'amicizia tra Castiglione e Raffaello*. Rome: Viella.

Ragno, T. (2011). Verità e conoscenza nel pensiero di Nicola Cusano. PhD dissertation. University of Verona.

Rauty, N. (2003). *Pistoia: Città e territorio nel medioevo*. Pistoia: Società pistoiese di storia patria.

Reguin, O. (2018). De l'abandon des mesures agraires romaines à l'établissement de modules géométriques médiévaux. *Histoire & Mesure* 33(1): 61–84.

Repishti, F. (2007). Architetti e ingegneri comunali, ducali e camerali nella Milano sforzesca e spagnola. In P. Bossi, S. Langé, and F. Repishti, eds., *Ingegneri ducali e camerali nel Ducato e nello Stato di Milano (1450–1706)*. Florence: Edifir, pp. 23–30.

Riccardi, P. (1870). *Biblioteca Matematica Italiana*. Modena: Erede Soliani.

Ristow, W. and Skelton, R. A. (1977). *Nautical Charts on Vellum in the Library of Congress*. Washington, DC: Library of Congress.

Rocca, P. (1871). *Pesi e misure antiche di Genova e del genovesato*. Genoa: Real Istituto sordo-muti.

Romano, D. (2015). *Markets and Marketplaces in Medieval Italy, c. 1100 to 1440*. New Haven, CT: Yale University Press.

Rowan, S. (1984). Reformatio Iuris and Luther's Reformation: Comment on the Lutheran Reformation and German Law. *Valparaiso University Law Review* 18(3): 631–42.

Rowland, I. D. (1998). *The Culture of the High Renaissance: Ancients and Moderns in Sixteenth-Century Rome*. Cambridge: Cambridge University Press.

Rubinstein, N. (1958). An Unknown Letter by Jacopo di Poggio Bracciolini on Discoveries of Classical Texts. *Italia Medievale Umanistica* 1: 383–400.

Ruggiero, G. (2015). *The Renaissance in Italy: A Social and Cultural History of the Rinascimento*. Cambridge: Cambridge University Press.

Ruiz, E. (1976). Los años Romanos y obras. *Cuadernos de Filología Clásica* 10: 189–247.

Russell. B. (1990). On the Relations of Number and Quantity. In N. Griffin and A. C. Lewis, eds., *The Collected Papers of Bertrand Russell*. Vol. 2: *The Philosophical Papers 1896–99*. Milton Park: Routledge, pp. 68–82.

Rykwert, J. (1996). *The Dancing Column: On Order in Architecture*. Boston, MA: MIT Press.

Saiber, A. (2017). *Measured Words: Computation and Writing in Renaissance Italy*. Toronto: Toronto University Press.

Salvestrini, F. (2010). L'alluvione fiorentina del 1333. In M. Matheus, G. Piccinni, G. Pinto, and G. M. Varanini, eds., *Le calamità ambientali nel tardo medioevo Europeo*. Florence: Firenze University Press, pp. 231–56.

Sangster, A., Stoner, G. N., and McCarthy, P. (2008). The Market for Luca Pacioli's *Summa Arithmetica*. *Accounting Historians Journal* 35(1): 111–34.

Santoro, C. (1961). *I registri delle lettere ducali del periodo sforzesco*. Milan: Castello sforzesco.

Scaglia, G. (1991). The "Colonnacce" of Forum Nervae As Cronaca's Inspiration for the "Cornicione" of Palazzo Strozzi. *Mitteilungen des Kunsthistorischen Institutes in Florence* 35(2/3): 153–70.

Scarpellini, F. (1811). *Prospetto delle operazioni fatte in Roma per lo stabilimento del nuovo sistema metrico negli Stati Romani*. Rome: De Romanis.

Scott, J. C. (1998) *Seeing Like a State: How Certain Schemes to Improve the Human Condition Have Failed*. New Haven, CT: Yale University Press.

Settia, A. A. (2008). *De re militari: Pratica e teoria nella guerra medievale*. Rome: Viella.

Sgarbi, C. (1993). A New Corpus of Vitruvian Images. *RES: Journal of Anthropology and Aesthetics* 23: 31–51.

Shearman, J. (2003) *Raphael in Early Modern Sources 1483–1602*. 2 vols. New Haven, CT: Yale University Press.

Silver, L. (1994). Power of the Press: Dürer's Arch of Honour. In I. Zdanowicz, ed., *Albrecht Dürer in the Collection of the National Gallery of Victoria*. Melbourne: National Gallery of Victoria, pp. 45–62.

Skemer, D. C. (2006). *Binding Words: Textual Amulets in the Middle Ages*. University Park: Pennsylvania State University Press.

Smith, A. M. (2014). *From Sight to Light: The Passage from Ancient to Modern Optics*. Chicago, IL: University of Chicago Press.

Smith, C. (1992). *Architecture in the Culture of Early Humanism: Ethics, Aesthetics, and eloquence, 1400–1470*. Oxford: Oxford University Press.

Smith, P. (2006). Laboratories. In K. Park and L. Daston, eds., *The Cambridge History on Science*. Cambridge: Cambridge University Press, pp. 290–305.

Spufford, P. (2003). *Power and Profit: The Merchant in Medieval Europe*. London: Thames & Hudson.

Stahl, A. (2012). The Making of a Gold Standard: The Ducat and Its Offspring, 1284–2001. In J. Munro, ed., *Money in the Pre-industrial World*. Cambridge: Cambridge University Press, pp. 45–62.

Stenhouse, W. (2005). *Reading Inscriptions and Writing Ancient History: Historical Scholarship in the Late Renaissance*. London: Institute of Classical Studies.

Stewart, S. (1993). *On Longing: Narratives of the Miniature, the Gigantic, the Souvenir, the Collection*. Durham, NC: Duke University Press.

Stinger, C. L. (1985). *The Renaissance in Rome*. Bloomington: Indiana University Press.

Summerson, J. (1980). *The Classical Language of Architecture*. London: Thames & Hudson.

Sznura, F. (1975). *L'espansione urbana di Firenze nel Dugento*. Florence: La Nuova Italia.

Tancon, I. (2005). *Lo scienziato Tito Livio Burattini (1617–1681) al servizio dei re di Polonia*. Trento: University of Trento.

Tangheroni, M. (1996). *Commercio e navigazione nel Medioevo*. Rome: Laterza.

Tavernor, R. (1998). *On Alberti and the Art of Building*. New Haven, CT: Yale University Press.

Tavernor, R. (2007). *Smoot's Ear: The Measure of Humanity*. New Haven, CT: Yale University Press.

Teller, P. (2013). The Concept of Measurement-Precision. *Synthese* 190(2): 189–202.

Timpanaro, S. (2005). *The Genesis of Lachmann's Method*. Chicago, IL: University of Chicago Press.

Tiriticco, L. (2013). La nuova teoria prospettica nei *Perspectivae libri sex*. In A. Becchi, D. Bertoloni Meli, and E. Gamba, eds., *Guidobaldo del Monte (1545–1607): Theory and Practice of the Mathematical Disciplines from Urbino to Europe*. Berlin. Editions Open Access, pp. 193–206.

Toneatto, L. (1994–95). *Codices artis mensoriae: I manoscritti degli antichi opuscoli latini d'agrimensura*. 3 vols. Spoleto: Centro italiano di studi sull'alto medioevo.

Tosi Brandi, E. (2017). *L'arte del sarto nel medioevo*. Bologna: Il Mulino.

Trachtenberg, M. (1985). Brunelleschi, Giotto and Rome. In A. Morrogh, F. Superbi Gioffredi, P. Morselli, and E. Borsook, eds., *Renaissance Studies in Honor of Craig Hugh Smyth*. Vol. 2 Florence: Giunti Barbera, pp. 675–97.

Trachtenberg, M. (1989). Perspective As Artistic Form: Optical Theory and Visual Culture from Giotto to Alberti. In S. Dupré, ed., *Perspective As Practice: Renaissance Cultures of Optics*. Turnhout: Brepols, pp. 19–70.

Trachtenberg, M. (1997). *Dominion of the Eye: Urbanism, Art, and Power in Early Modern Florence*. Cambridge: Cambridge University Press.

Tucci, U. (1973). The Psychology of the Venetian Merchant in the Sixteenth Century. In J. R. Hale, ed., *Renaissance Venice*. Totowa, NJ: Rowman and Littlefield, pp. 346–78.

Tucci, U. (1974). La metrologia storica. Qualche premessa metodologica. *Zbornik Odsjeka za povijesne znanosti Zavoda za povijesne i društvene znanosti Hrvatske akademije znanosti i umjetnosti* 7: 305–18.

Tucci, U. (1990–91). Benedetto Cotrugli, Raguseo e il suo *Libro dell'arte di mercatura*. *Atti e Memorie della Società Dalmata di Storia Patria* 3: 1–12.

Terjanian, P., ed., *The Last Knight: The Art, Armor, and Ambition of Maximilian I*. New York: Metropolitan Museum of Art, 2019.

Ulivi, E. (2015). Masters, Questions and Challenges in the Abacus Schools. *Archive for the History of Exact Sciences* 69(6): 651–70.

Ungers, O. M. (1994). "Ordo, pondo et mensura": Criteri architettonici del Rinascimento. In H. Milton and V. Magnano Lampugnani, eds., *Rinascimento: da Brunelleschi a Michelangelo: La rappresentazione dell'architettura*. Milan: Bompiani, pp. 307–17.

Uzielli, G. (1899). *Le misure lineari medievali medioevali e l'effige di Cisto*. Florence: Seeber.

Vagenheim, G. (2011). La falsificazione epigrafica nell'Italia della seconda metà del Cinquecento. In J. Carbonell Manils, H. Gimeno Pascual, and J. L. Moraljo Álvarez, eds., *El monumento epigráfico en contextos secundarios: Procesos de reutilización, interpretación y falsificación.* Barcelona: Universitat Autònoma de Barcelona, pp. 217–26.

Vagnetti, L. (1974). Lo studio di Roma negli scritti albertiani. In *Convegno internazionale indetto nel V centenario di Leon Battista Alberti.* Rome: Accademia dei Lincei, pp. 73–140.

Valle, C. A. (1855). *Storia di Alessandria.* Turin: Falletti.

Vasoli, C. (1977). *I miti e gli astri.* Naples: Guida.

Verbaal, W. (2016). The Vitruvian Middle Ages and Beyond. *Arethusa* 49(2): 215–25.

Vérin, H. (1993). *La gloire des ingénieurs.* Paris: Albin Michel.

Wassell, S. R. (2010). Commentary on the ex ludi rerum mathematicorum. In K. Williams, L. March, and S. R. Wassell, eds., *The Mathematical Works of Leon Battista Alberti.* Basel: Springer, pp. 75–140.

Weiss, E. (1988). *The Renaissance Discovery of Classical Antiquity.* Oxford: Blackwell.

Welch, E. (2005). *Shopping in the Renaissance: Consumer Cultures in Italy, 1400–1600.* New Haven, CT: Yale University Press.

White, J. (1972). *The Birth and Rebirth of Pictorial Space.* London: Faber and Faber.

Williams, K. and Bevilacqua, M. G. (2013). Leon Battista Alberti's Bombarda Problem in Ludi Matematici. *Mathematical Intelligencer* 35(4): 27–38.

Wittkower, R. (1944). Principles of Palladio's Architecture. *Journal of the Warburg and Courtauld Institutes* 7: 102–22.

Yamey, B. S. (1989). *Art and Accounting.* New Haven, CT: Yale University Press.

Yerkes, C. (2013). *Drawing after Architecture: Renaissance Architectural Drawings and Their Reception.* Venice: Marsilio.

Yoder, J. G. (1988) *Unrolling Time: Christiaan Huygens and the Mathematization of Nature.* Cambridge: Cambridge University Press.

Zampa, P. (2010). Il Codice Strozzi: alcune considerazioni. *Opus incertum* 5: 65–75.

Zanetti, C. (2017). *Janello Torriani and the Spanish Empire.* Leiden: Brill.

Zangheri, L. (1987). Firenze e la Toscana nel periodo napoleonico: Progetti e realizzazioni. In *Villes et territoire pendant la période napoléonienne.* Rome, École Française, pp. 315–25.

Zöllner, F. (1995). L'uomo vitruviano di Leonardo da Vinci, Rudolf Wittkower e L'Angelus Novus di Walter Benjamin. *Raccolta Vinciana* 26: 329–58.

Cambridge Elements ⹀

# The Renaissance

## John Henderson
*Birkbeck, University of London, and Wolfson College, University of Cambridge*

John Henderson is Emeritus Professor of Italian Renaissance History at Birkbeck, University of London, and Emeritus Fellow of Wolfson College, University of Cambridge. His recent publications include *Florence Under Siege: Surviving Plague in an Early Modern City* (2019), and *Plague and the City*, edited with Lukas Engelmann and Christos Lynteris (2019), and *Representing Infirmity: Diseased Bodies in Renaissance Italy*, edited with Fredrika Jacobs and Jonathan K. Nelson (2021). He is also the author of *Piety and Charity in Late Medieval Florence* (1994); *The Great Pox: The French Disease in Renaissance Europe*, with Jon Arrizabalaga and Roger French (1997); and *The Renaissance Hospital: Healing the Body and Healing the Soul* (2006). Forthcoming publications include a Cambridge Element, *Representing and Experiencing the Great Pox in Renaissance Italy* (2023).

## Jonathan K. Nelson

Jonathan K. Nelson teaches Italian Renaissance Art at Syracuse University Florence and is research associate at the Harvard Kennedy School. His books include *Filippino Lippi* (2004, with Patrizia Zambrano); *Leonardo e la reinvenzione della figura femminile* (2007), *The Patron's Payoff: Conspicuous Commissions in Italian Renaissance Art* (2008, with Richard J. Zeckhauser), *Filippino Lippi* (2022); and he co-edited *Representing Infirmity. Diseased Bodies in Renaissance Italy* (2021). He co-curated museum exhibitions dedicated to Michelangelo (2002), Botticelli and Filippino (2004), Robert Mapplethorpe (2009), and Marcello Guasti (2019), and two online exhibitions about Bernard Berenson (2012, 2015). Forthcoming publications include a Cambridge Element, *Risks in Renaissance Art: Production, Purchase, Reception* (2023).

## Assistant Editor
Sarah McBryde, *Birkbeck, University of London*

## Editorial Board
Wendy Heller, *Scheide Professor of Music History, Princeton University*
Giorgio Riello, *Chair of Early Modern Global History, European University Institute, Florence*
Ulinka Rublack, *Professor of Early Modern History, St Johns College, University of Cambridge*
Jane Tylus, *Andrew Downey Orrick Professor of Italian and Professor of Comparative Literature, Yale University*

## About the Series
Timely, concise, and authoritative, Elements in the Renaissance showcases cutting-edge scholarship by both new and established academics. Designed to introduce students, researchers, and general readers to key questions in current research, the volumes take multi-disciplinary and transnational approaches to explore the conceptual, material, and cultural frameworks that structured Renaissance experience.

Cambridge Elements ≡

# The Renaissance

## Elements in the Series

Printed in the United States
by Baker & Taylor Publisher Services